Lederman

The Demystification
of **Yap**

The Demystification of **Yap**

Dialectics of Culture
on a
Micronesian Island

David Labby

University of Chicago Press
Chicago and London

DAVID LABBY received his Ph.D. in anthropology
at the University of Chicago. He has taught at
Portland Community College in Oregon and is
currently doing independent research on the
American working class.

The University of Chicago Press, Chicago 60637
The University of Chicago Press, Ltd., London

©1976 by The University of Chicago
All rights reserved. Published 1976
Printed in the United States of America
80 79 78 77 76   9 8 7 6 5 4 3 2 1

Library of Congress Cataloging in Publication Data

Labby, David.
  The demystification of Yap.

  Includes bibliographical references and index.
  1. Ethnology—Yap, Caroline Islands. 2. Kin-
ship—Yap, Caroline Islands. 3. Land tenure—Yap,
Caroline Islands. I. Title.
GN671.C3L3   301.29'96'6   75-21270
ISBN 0-226-46711-2

"A Song from Kanif against the New Customs" (p. vii)
was collected by Wilhelm Müller (1917) during the years
of the German occupation of Yap (1899–1914), when the
first effective colonial administration of Yapese affairs
was established. By this time much of the traditional life
had already been undermined by depopulation.

To David Schneider, without whose continuing support this book would not have been written, and to the Yapese—Moorow, Tamagtamdad, Faimaw, Waath, Muut, Pinnifen, Figir, Mfeg, Kenmed, Mangabachan, Barwahr, Saling, Gamangang, Dapoy, Duwer, Leon, Tinagchugen, Mana', Galinmagar, Wag, and so many others—who helped us and taught us about Yap.

Kum magaragath!

A Song from Kanif against the New Customs

Composed by Tamag

Wait! We the spirits of this land
Wish to state our case, yo!

I have come to ask
I have come to ask
What has happened that things have gone bad
What has happened that things have gone bad
With the people of Rull and Tamil?
What has happened that you have hurried into this?
You are unfortunate, yo!
You have fallen into poverty, yo!
Greed has fallen on this land.
What has happened that you have hurried into this?
You are unfortunate, yo!
When greed overcomes you
Then you impoverish each other.
Have you profit in mind?
Have you profit in hand?
You are unfortunate, yo!

When the new seeds come up
Come up here on this land
They bring humiliation
Humiliation of Yap
That only the Administrator should speak with authority.
If he sees a person whose purpose is good
He will let him be.
If he sees a person whose purpose is bad
He will exile him.

Honor! What is honor for?
The gods go unhonored in the shrines.

Let people go worship them
Humbling themselves before the gods.
Let us stand up again.
We are poor because our canoe is shattered
Shattered.
Our own rivalry has foundered our canoe.
We are at the end.
We have suffered the end.
We trouble ourselves in vain
For our rights here on earth
When they are impossible for us.

We are impoverished!

Contents

Foreword

The idea that culture can best be understood as a system of symbols and meanings has gained wide recognition during the last decade, and a number of works of very high quality have been based on this formulation. This book takes its place among the best of them, for it is an extraordinarily sensitive symbolic analysis of the culture of Yap, a high island in the West Caroline Islands of Micronesia.

Central to Labby's analysis is the place of land in Yapese culture. Since land is among the epitomizing symbols of so many Oceanic cultures (and cultures throughout the world), this analysis will prove useful far beyond the shores of Yap.

But Labby has taken the analysis one step further than usual. The task for most students of culture is to establish and formulate or translate the native categories and concepts to show their total structure. Labby has gone on to ask why things are structured in that particular way. There is thus a systematic attempt to relate the cultural analysis to other phenomena, most particularly the mode of production, and thereby to account for the particular way Yapese culture is structured. Land therefore comes into the analysis at one level as one of the epitomizing symbols and at another as the primary mode of production, and the interplay between these two meanings of land is a central focus of the analysis.

Labby applies some important Marxist concepts to what is basically a noncapitalistic society. This direction of analysis is becoming more and more important in the thinking of an increasing number of anthropologists today. The skill with which Labby applies these Marxist concepts is an important contribution to the book, though the major value lies precisely in the conjunction of the sensitive analysis of Yapese culture with the attempt to move toward a Marxist analysis.

David M. Schneider

Acknowledgments

I am not the first anthropologist to study Yapese culture, and I have been fortunate in being able to refer to the work of others. The starting point for this study was, in fact, the work of David M. Schneider, which was based on his own research on Yap in 1947-48. It was in talking with David Schneider during my student days at the University of Chicago that I first became interested in Yap, and my own work has essentially been a continuation of what he began. Since it would be impossible to acknowledge in the text all the points where I am indebted to him, I will simply acknowledge my general debt here.

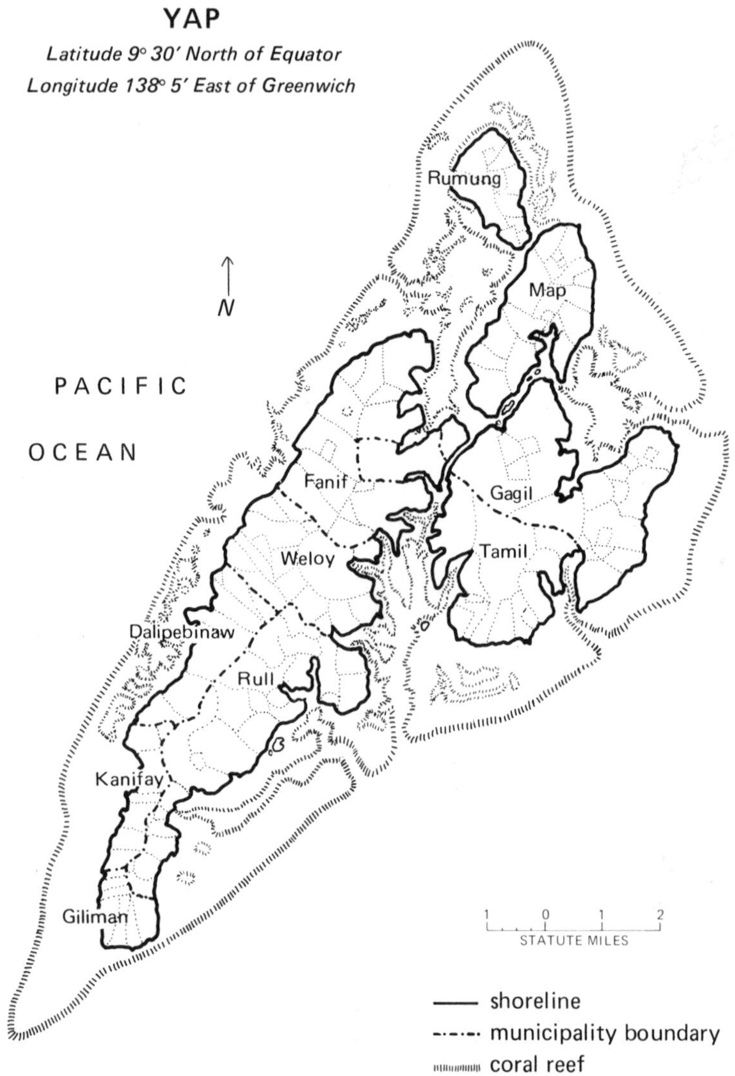

YAP

Latitude 9° 30' North of Equator
Longitude 138° 5' East of Greenwich

↑
N

PACIFIC

OCEAN

Rumung

Map

Fanif

Gagil

Weloy

Tamil

Dalipebinaw

Rull

Kanifay

Giliman

```
1      0      1      2
STATUTE MILES
```

— shoreline
-·-·- municipality boundary
ılıılıılı coral reef
·········· village boundary

Map 1

1 Introduction

The island of Yap lies in the Western Caroline Islands of Micronesia and is part of the Trust Territory of the Pacific Islands, a possession granted to the United States as a "strategic trust" by the United Nations after World War II. Yap itself is a high island, the raised edge of a submarine ridge, divided in four places by minor waterways and an excavated canal. Although the island is not large in any comparative sense, comprising only some thirty-seven square miles, it is large enough and varied enough topographically so that it can easily assume its own imposing spatial and social dimensions. The island once contained about 130 villages and was divided into a dozen rival chiefdoms, each trying to advance its own interests through warfare and constant political maneuvering, and each having its own variants of language and custom. At the time of the fieldwork on which this study was based (summer 1969, and March 1970 to June 1971), Yapese life was still divided, but by then the important division had come to be between the westernized town of Colonia, situated at Yap's central harbor and the site of colonial administration for approximately one hundred years, and the outlying villages, some of which were still fairly isolated and retained at least some of the traditional practices and beliefs.

Nothing certain is known of the early history of Yap—neither where the various peoples who became the Yapese originated nor when they arrived on the island. We do know, however, that the culture is of considerable antiquity. Archeological excavations on Yap have unearthed samples of charcoal that have been radiocarbon dated to around A.D. 176 (Gifford 1959, p. 195), a time depth that is also reflected in the highly distinctive Yapese cultural and linguistic patterns. Whatever their origins and whatever customs the settlers of Yap brought with them, they had time to develop a language and culture unique to the island. According to Yapese tradition, there have been a succession of political and cultural orders on Yap, with power shifting from one part of the island to another and new

1

religious and social forms being established. It is interesting that, according to the radiocarbon dates, a chief named Rigog, who was said to have been a founder of the present indigenous order, lived only two hundred years ago (Gifford 1959, p. 195).

Contact with the Western world may have started as early as 1526. First contacts seem by recorded evidence to have been infrequent, at intervals ranging from 50 to 150 years, and Yapese society did not suffer direct colonial interference until the late 1800s. Yet, already by that time the effect of the early Western presence, mainly in the form of diseases it introduced in the area, appears to have been devastating. Estimates of Yap's traditional population, based on a count of surviving house foundations, have run as high as 50,000 persons, though a figure between 28,000 and 34,000 appears to be more reasonable (Schneider 1956). When the first census of Yap was conducted by the Catholic mission in 1899, however, the population had been reduced to 7,808 persons—and it would decline even more in the years to come.

The Yapese reacted to this decimation in the only way they could. Ten years before the census a Spanish Capuchin priest, Father Arbacegui, a member of the first missionary group on Yap, had written an account of a revival of a fertility cult by seven men who lived on Mount Matsebap:

> It was said that any woman who ascended the mountain and left an offering to the god would conceive a child. The priest notes that these superstitions received their just desert—first, the wives of five of the seven self-styled "missionaries" died; then disaster befell many of the women who had visited the seers. One died in child-birth, another had a miscarriage, a third gave birth to a child who was so sickly that he died a few days later. In a short time, the fertility cult proved to be quite the reverse and word spread among the Yapese that if a woman went to Matsebap her child would surely die (Hezel 1970, p. 10).

Ironically, the failure of the cult ultimately helped the Capuchin mission buy the land of the shrine on Matsebap for a nominal fee (90,000 square meters for 12 pesos), and there they built their own church (Hezel 1970, p. 11).

The process of depopulation had, of course, definite effects on Yapese culture. When the German Wilhelm Müller was doing his ethnography in 1908, he found that depopulation had irreparably upset the process of the hereditary transmission of ritual information and priestly position and that the Yapese religious system was in a state of near collapse.

Westerners themselves were not significantly present around Yap until the 1850s, when traders were drawn to the area in search of copra and of trepang, a sea slug the Chinese considered a great delicacy. From that point on, the history of Yap became more and more tightly tied to the history of the Western world. In 1869, as part of the German commercial expansion throughout Oceania, a trading station was established on Yap by the J. C. Godeffroy and Son Company. Increasing German presence in the area threatened the Spanish claim to the Caroline Islands, and in 1885 the Spaniards attempted to secure their claim by founding an administrative settlement on Yap. On 26 August after spending almost a week finding a suitable place to unload their animals (riding horses, buffalo, oxen, etc.) and the shipload of stones they had brought to build a church and a governor's residence, the Spanish finally decided to have the formal celebration of their occupation of the island on the next day, inviting all foreign residents. That very evening, however, a German ship raced in and, amid a din of beating drums and loud cries, immediately hoisted the German flag on Yap, claiming the Carolines for the Kaiser. According to an observer, "the dumbfounded Spanish were thunderstruck" (Kubary, quoted in Müller 1917). The dispute rising out of this comedy was submitted to Pope Leo XIII for arbitration. He conferred sovereignty on the Spanish but enjoined them to allow the Germans to establish trading and commercial enterprises. The Spanish immediately set about building churches and attempting to convert the population to Catholicism. In 1899, however, after Spain had lost the Spanish-American War, Germany purchased the Carolines and the Marianas to complete its Oceanic empire, establishing its own administration on Yap.

In line with their commercial interests, the Germans set about modernizing the means of communication on Yap. They reorganized the traditional political units into administrative districts that could provide an adequate labor force, and they built roads, a major canal linking the distant northern areas with Colonia, and a cable station. It was said that the Germans also dug up many of the painstakingly laid stone pathways that had paved the villages and run throughout Yap because they found that their horses stumbled and slipped on them.

The Germans set up their own system of regulations and trained a Yapese police force and army. Warfare was forbidden, all but neutralizing the complex Yapese political system that formerly had functioned to keep the different district powers on Yap balanced against each other through intricate networks of alliances and counteralliances. As the traditional Yapese political system came to be effectively replaced, it began to lose its coherence and force. Traditional chiefs were used by the German authorities in their administration, but this hardly gave them the power and initiative in directing the affairs of Yap that they had formerly exercised.

The German administration strongly encouraged copra production but was hindered in its efforts by an insect blight introduced from the Phillippines and by a series of droughts and typhoons. At first cultivation of the coconut palms and preparation of the dried coconut meat was left to individual Yapese working on their own lands. But in 1912 the Jaluit Company, formed in 1887 by an amalgamation of the leading German mercantile firms, began to extend its operations from the Eastern Carolines to the west in order to bring copra production under unified control. It planned to obtain thirty-year leases on land that had been purchased by the government and to establish plantations to be operated with local labor. The beginning of World War I brought a halt to the project. The last German census (1911) put the population of Yap at 6,187 persons.

In 1914 the Japanese, taking advantage of the outbreak of World War I to follow their own plans for the area, seized control of Yap and the rest of German Micronesia. Japanese commercial penetration into the area had begun as early as 1890 when Ukichi Taguchi launched a project to help jobless samurai, who had lost their livelihood with the dissolution of the feudal system, by resettling them as merchants in the South Sea islands. The project never went beyond an initial voyage to Guam, Yap, Palau, and Ponape to establish trade. Other Japanese traders followed, however, and by 1912 approximately one-third of the trade in the Marianas and Western Carolines was with Japan, and more than half the foreign occupants of the area were Japanese. With the end of the German occupation in 1914, Japanese business rapidly forced other foreign interests from the area. In 1920 Japan was confirmed in its possession of Micronesia under a mandate from the League of Nations.

The extensive Japanese commercial development of the mandated

Two girls dressed in newly made grass
skirts. The skirts were made of all
different kinds of foliage—betal fronds,
banana leaf, hibiscus bark, and so forth.
Skirts for younger women were generally
greener and more fragrant.

The cutting of the young children's hair in a ceremony called "cutting off the hands of the spirit" (*thab pa' e kan*). With this first haircut the spirit (*mam*) who had accompanied the child since its conception, giving it its physical features and protecting it in its early life, was said to leave. The ceremony was done when the child was old enough to walk and to care for itself.

Chewing betel nut in a moment of quiet, a young wife cares for her young children and those of the other members of the extended family while the other women tend their gardens.

Leon of Magachugil village and his son

Women doing a sitting line dance. The
wide, stiff, light-colored bands are
young coconut fronds. The white rosettes
are made of toilet paper.

A traditional Yapese house

A man dividing up fish after the village
fishing expedition. He wears the hibiscus-fiber belt (*kofor*) signifying
manhood.

The young girls' (*rugoth*) quarters. The thatching on the ground is being prepared to reroof the buildings after a typhoon.

Women singing during an intervillage competitive exchange (*tayor*). The danced song requested goods from the host villages which had previously been able to request goods from the singers' village in a similar exchange.

A group of high-school students. As a
sign of increased maturity the boys wear
two loincloths (*thu*), one red and one
white.

area had only a limited effect on Yap. Although large sugar plantations were established on Saipan, employing Japanese labor almost exclusively, and fishing, mining, and farming were established elsewhere, the resources of Yap were found to have little potential. Farming and mining were tried but were deemed unprofitable. Although there developed on the island a fairly sizable Japanese colony centered around administrative and commercial activities, the Yapese had little part in it. A few jobs as government employees, domestic servants, or employees with Japanese business concerns were available, but in 1937 the officially reported figures for Yap District (Yap Island plus the outlying atolls) show only 4 percent of the local population engaged in such occupations.[1] Until World War II, at least, the Yapese appear to have been involved rather peripherally in the Japanese economic system, acting mainly as individual producers of copra and continuing to follow a basically traditional pattern of domestic life.

The Japanese did not hide the fact that they felt the Yapese were vastly inferior, and they gave little consideration to the local culture. The parts of the intricate yearly cycle of village and district religious rituals during which Yapese were to refrain from labor for periods of up to a month were prohibited by the Japanese because they interfered with work. The remaining rituals were eventually abandoned by the Yapese themselves. Attendance at a five-year school in Japanese language was mandatory. In school, as in everything else, the Japanese maintained a harsh and uncompromising discipline. The Yapese were required to labor at the tasks appointed to them by the administration, some being sent to plantations and mines outside of Yap proper. With the military buildup of the mandated islands before and during World War II, Yapese laborers were used much more intensively than they previously had been and were put to work building airfields and other installations.

The Japanese are remembered with mixed feelings on Yap, for in the end they were reduced to a plight worse than that of the Yapese. The older people tell of how, toward the end of the war, the Japanese ran out of food supplies and had to subsist on anything they could find or steal. They had so little, it was said, they were reduced to eating small hermit crabs and even lizards. But the Yapese also remember how their own elaborately built houses and canoes were broken up for firewood, how stone house foundations and even some traditional stone money were used in construction works, how the magnificent men's houses and meeting houses were torn down so

that they would not be spotted by the enemy as centers of population, and how they had to leave their homes and live in the safety of
the central hills. The first census (1946) after the American takeover
√ placed the population at 2,582 persons.

In 1945 the United States assumed control of Micronesia. For the
first six years, American rule was exercised by the United States
Navy, which followed a policy of minimal interference in Yapese
affairs. Rather than using forced labor as the Japanese had, the
Americans attracted a small labor force by paying wages and so
reconstructed the roads and built a hospital. They set up an
elementary school system and attempted to establish, with no
success, a Parent-Teacher Association and a father's council. Elec-
tions were held for the position of chief in the different districts, and
the traditional high-ranking chiefs were duly elected. These chiefs
were to act as liaison between the navy and the Yapese population,
helping to distribute goods and mobilize labor, as well as enforcing
navy policy, acting as judges in their districts, and relaying navy
lectures on the need for sanitation, education, and public orderli-
ness. Much to the consternation of the navy, however, the liaisons
were generally unable to do these things, because the rationale
behind the chiefs' traditional authority had long since disappeared
√ and they had little effective power. The Americans did not intervene
in traditional Yapese affairs. Some religious and ritual practices
were revived, and a few men's houses, individual residences, and
canoes were rebuilt in the traditional style (Lingenfelter 1971, pp.
273–82).

When the administration of the area was transferred to the United
States Department of Interior in 1951, however, it became increasingly clear that changes were occurring that made a return to
traditional cultural patterns unlikely. The administration bureau-
cracy and public services opened many salaried positions that could
be occupied by Yapese. As these and other job opportunities
increased, more people moved to town and acquired a taste for
imported consumer goods. Whereas the Japanese had outlawed the
consumption of alcoholic beverages, the Americans only expressed
strong disapproval. In 1956 the importation of beer was approved by
referendum, and a quota of five hundred cases a month was
established. The quota was quickly raised to one thousand cases a
month, and then, as waiting lists appeared, prices rose, and people
began guzzling their purchases before too many friends arrived, the
quota system was dropped altogether in hopes that consumption

would level off. It did not. Nor did the purchase of any other consumer goods level off as the improved shipping and air facilities encouraged their import and the United States yearly increased its allocation of funds to the Trust Territory. The new consumer economy was an extremely strong argument for abandoning traditional patterns and following the opportunities opened up by the Americans. Under the Department of the Interior's administration, the local elected chiefs became "magistrates" who formed their own council (dominated by American administrators) that dealt with such problems as taxation, municipal ordinances, law enforcement, and labor mobilization (Lingenfelter 1971, pp. 273–82). Activity focused more and more on the culture the Americans were introducing and less and less on traditional Yapese affairs.

From the beginning of my stay on Yap, it was clear that the traditional culture I had gone to study was rapidly being abandoned. Some of the Yapese still wore traditional dress, but that did not disguise the fundamental changes that were occurring. Colonia had replaced the villages as the focal point of the society. A large portion of the population had moved there, and the few stores, government buildings, and residences that were its nucleus had become surrounded by clusters of small shacks, many of which were made of scrap metal and discarded packing crates. Many other people commuted to work by car and bus. There were dirt roads through much of the island, and the Yapese had come to see the advantages of cars, which were being bought as fast as they could be imported. While the women continued to support their families with food from the village, taro patches, and hillside gardens, the men were doing less fishing and more wage labor, providing their families with a little money to buy such store goods as canned fish or corned beef and spending the rest on beer and liquor, which they consumed in great quantities. Everyone had accepted the necessity of money, even if only for buying sugar, kerosene, cigarettes, and matches. The government had established a school system on an American model with a high school (Yap High School—"Home of the Eagles") centrally located just outside Colonia. Drunkenness and juvenile delinquency were common.

There was no general sentiment among the Yapese against these changes. Living conditions were definitely improving and the population expanding—the census of 1970 showed 4,594 persons. But prospects for the future seemed depressing. As the population shifted to wage work and a money-oriented economy, demanding more and more consumer goods, little effort was being made to develop local economic resources. The Yapese were being brought into the modern world by appropriations of money from the United States, which was interested in Micronesia because of its strategic military proximity to Southeast Asia and the Orient.

Imports for the fiscal year ending 30 June 1970 had reached $852,800 whereas exports were only $18,100, an import-export ratio of roughly 47:1. Nor was Yap the exception in the Trust Territory. The "Report of the United Nations Visiting Mission to the Trust Territory of the Pacific Islands, 1970" contains the following warning:

> The Territory is obviously living beyond its means. In 1968, 95 percent of its budget was derived from grants by the Administering Authority. . . .
>
> In external trade, this artificial situation is reflected in a serious imbalance which is growing worse. While exports, which are sensitive to fluctuations in world copra prices, remain stationary (1964—$2.6 million; 1966—$3 million; 1968—$3.02 million; 1969—$2.85 million), imports are increasing rapidly (1964—$5.6 million; 1966—$8.9 million; 1968—$13.5 million; 1969—$13.9 million). Most of these imports consist of consumer goods, particularly food stuffs, which in 1969 accounted for $5.7 million in imports, much of which could be produced locally. Such a trend in no way encourages the population to make the maximum use of the Territory's own resources but leads it to rely increasingly on purchase of foreign products, financed from outside. Obviously, this situation has repercussions at the political level. [P. 34]

As Micronesians began to debate their political status vis-à-vis the United States, the repercussions of such economic dependency were indeed becoming obvious. Nevertheless, few people on Yap seemed upset by this predicament and what it implied. The Yapese appeared generally more concerned with taking advantage of the new economic opportunities opened up by the American administration —the new wage-paying jobs and the new consumer goods.

As people were faced with surviving in the world of jobs and a consumer economy, much of the traditional culture I wanted to study had become of little importance to them, and less and less of such information was being transmitted between generations. But there were still older people who were knowledgeable in traditional matters, and it was with them that I worked. Not much attention was being paid anymore to the old people, who represented a world that was quickly being left behind, and many of them were as grateful to me for the attention and company I provided as I was grateful to them for putting up with me, a strange American who would suddenly appear carrying a Yapese betel-nut basket full of note-books and asking highly specific questions about things long unmentioned. They provided a description of traditional Yapese life as they had been allowed to live it under the Germans and Japanese and, in many cases, continue to live it to the extent that they are able under the Americans.

By the nature of the situation, the traditional life that people described was predominantly domestic, limited to the concerns of family, family relations, and subsistence. People had still followed the traditional marriage, residence, and kinship patterns, as well as a system of regulations and eating classes that operated around the notions of "purity" (*tabugul*) and "impurity" (*taay*). The mainstay of the diet had remained taro (mainly *Cyrtosperma chamissonis*), a starchy root grown by the women in wet, muddy, dug-out patches near the coast; this was supplemented by vegetables from hillside slash-and-burn gardens, primarily yams (mainly *Dioscorea alata, Dioscorea esculenta,* and *Dioscorea nummulacia*) and introduced varieties of sweet potatoes. The men provided fish from the lagoon, caught in various traps or nets or, when they became available, with metal spears. But the villages that many people had once lived in were no longer crowded with neatly fenced peaked Yapese houses, massive community centers, and men's houses, nor was there still the elaborate division of labor that had once assigned specific duties and obligations to each separate household estate. With a depopula-tion of over 90 percent, most of the estates in the village were abandoned, and whatever specialized functions they had had were forgotten or appended to the prerogatives of remaining estates. The once populous and highly organized villages were reduced to small groups of families living here and there amid the dense tropical vege-tation and scores of overgrown house foundations. Many villages died out entirely or were deserted as their members moved to better land. Although the people I talked with certainly knew of the traditional political alliance system and had seen it used to whatever extent possible in dealings with the different administrations, none had witnessed it in full operation, and comparatively little of it had remained intact. Likewise, the distinctions of the multilevel village stratification system were still recognized, though they had become somewhat blurred. Almost nothing was known of traditional reli-gious beliefs.

I have therefore had to base this study primarily on an analysis of

✓ domestic relations. This limitation, however, has not been without advantages. It was precisely the domestic and productive relations that were fundamental to Yapese survival, the relations through which the Yapese produced and reproduced their culture. A close description of these relations does, I think, provide us with basic insights into the nature of that culture, with respect not only to its specific form but also to the conditions that gave it that form.

What I have tried to do, first of all, is to describe the process of Yapese society—the relations of landholding, kinship, status, power, and so forth—using the terms the Yapese themselves used in their explanations to me; by this method I have hoped to present, to the extent that I could, the Yapese's own ideas as to the nature of relations in their society. One might call this a description of "Yapese social theory," though this tends to make it seem as if such ideas were already much more abstracted from experience than in fact they were. The Yapese did not provide me with an organized account of their culture, but they did respond patiently and with interest to my questions as I expanded and tested my understanding of what they said.

In connection with this, I have further tried to show that the Yapese's explanations of their social relations have a fundamental validity; that they reflect in a very real sense the Yapese's own historical life process. Traditional Yapese culture is, to be sure, initially mystifying. It is a realm of ancestral spirits, totemic clans, kinship networks, "pure" and "impure" people and land, village eating classes, ranked villages, and elaborate political alliances. The problem, as with any other cultural phenomenon, is to demystify these constructs—neither to accept them by a leap of faith nor to justify them by simply finding their logical coherence or formal structure, but rather to understand them concretely as the products of a specific human reality. The problem here is to understand Yapese cultural constructs ultimately as the categories of a particular material and social situation, as categories created by and within that situation. A "cultural analysis" that attempts to define the way a people *think* but ignores the way people *live,* in the very tasks of survival that face them daily, seems to me to be significantly misconceived. For it is only as we begin to comprehend statements as the testimony of a particular people in a particular space and time that we can also begin to define what they mean with any accuracy and completeness. In this sense there is, properly speaking, no such thing as a distinct or separate "cultural analysis."

Admittedly, my own analysis here operates only at the most general level. There was much that the people I talked to could not tell me because it was not within their experience. Their own lives had been depoliticized and limited to the extent that it is probably possible to get only the broadest understanding of the dynamics of traditional Yapese culture from their accounts. But there was also much that I simply failed to ask about or did not observe carefully. Being anxious to grasp the main structural features of Yapese culture, I tended to ignore the ways that structure was played out in individual personal life and so recorded virtually no case histories or observational material. It is clear now, too, that I should have done a much closer and more systematic study of Yapese agricultural practice. Still, the analysis does, I hope, at least outline the dimensions of a concrete comprehension of Yapese traditional culture, however generalized and tentative it must remain.

My account of Yapese cultural constructs forms the main body of the book; the historical interpretation of them occurs in chapter 7. Although a general grasp of the ethnographic material is necessary if the last chapter is to be comprehensible, the reader who is not interested in the intricacies of Yapese kinship relations and the terms for kinsmen might skim over or skip chapter 5, "The People of Estate."

I should finally note that although the analysis uses the terms of historical materialism—of the dialectic between historical form and material necessity, between the social relations of production and the material forces of production—I did not set out to "do" a Marxist analysis of Yapese traditional culture. I began simply with a dissatisfaction with Lévi-Straussian structuralism and the kind of formalism that seems to be able to resolve itself only in the "structure of the mind," thus providing little insight into the specific content of human history. But I had only the vaguest notion of how this could be overcome or what doing so would mean. In that I have now come to an understanding of historical materialism, it has been to an important extent through the process of working with the Yapese material, because that material has seemed to demand it. Although this has been for me an important exercise, the initial lack of critical self-consciousness has, I think, distinctly limited the study, making it somewhat abstract and mechanical. I would hesitate to call this a "Marxist" analysis of Yapese traditional culture, but at the same time I would hope that it was in the process of becoming one.

2 The People and the Land

The people of traditional Yap lived as they worked the land and sea, the resources their ancestors had worked and developed since long before. The island of Yap itself, as well as the sea area within the barrier reef surrounding it, had been totally transformed for them by the continuous labor of a growing population. The major taro patches and gardens had been laid out; the stone fish traps in the sea, I was told, had been built in all the places they would be effective. Every piece of land, every tree, every bit of fishing area within the reef was owned. The pressure on resources had already become an important factor in Yapese life. With only some thirty-seven square miles of land and a population of about 30,000 persons, there had long ago ceased to be any unclaimed land on which a person might settle. In many places people had attempted to extend their living space by constructing extensive fills at the ocean side—a process requiring massive labor, given their simple technology. Others had simply been left landless. These the Yapese describe as a population of *malethay,* people without land, going from house to house for food, depending on the bounty of landed relatives.

Competition for land on Yap had become acute not only because of population increase but also because not all land was equally fertile and productive. Yap is a high island divided into distinct ecological zones. Most of the 130 or so traditional villages were close to the shoreline, behind dense entanglements of mangrove that leave only an occasional open beach. There the land is fertile, and the villages stood amid a luxurious green enclosure of coconut, palm, banana, papaya, mango, breadfruit, betel, and tropical chestnut trees. In and around the villages were numerous wet taro patches, muddy pits excavated in the fertile alluvial soils of the coastal flats, inland depressions, and valley bottoms, and irrigated by channeled fresh water. They provided not only the basic staple of the traditional Yapese diet, producing taro year round, but also swarms of

12

mosquitoes that in traditional times could drive people to sleeping on rafts in the lagoon during a hot windless night.

Behind the villages, the land slopes upward to the central highlands. In the south, low, sweeping rises form inland hills that are covered with grass and pandanus trees and are fertile enough to support yam gardening. From there the hills lift to the steep, forested mountainous areas of central Yap and the extensive, though less productive, plateau of the north. In this latter region are areas of totally infertile badlands, barren land that is cut by large, flat-bottomed ravines and smaller sharp valleys. The slopes and ridges between the coastal living area and the central highlands were also used for yam and sweet potato gardens and, lower down, for some wet taro patches, except where the incline became too steep, as was the case among the hills of central Yap. During the rainy season (July through October), when about half of Yap's annual rainfall of around 120 inches occurs, these hillsides are green and moist, covered with a dense blanket of tropical vines and foliage. With the onset of the tradewinds and then the dry season (December through April) the green shades into brown, and soon one can hear the bursting sound of burning groves of bamboo as the women slash and burn plots here and there for their new upland gardens.

A geological survey carried out on Yap (Johnson, Alvis, and Hetzler 1960) makes it appear that only about half the land area of the island was suitable for cultivation, with a major part, approximately four-fifths, of that area limited to yam and sweet potato gardening and only the remaining fifth utilizable for growing wetland taro. It is likely that sweet potatoes were introduced through Western contact and that upland gardens were previously used mainly for yam cultivation, the poorer soils being fortified at times with compost and with earth removed from the pits dug for growing wet taro (Barrau 1961). Yet, although there has been no systematic survey to examine the extent to which the different land areas have been exploited, one has only to walk back though a village into the hills to discover, first, a complex of closely spaced abandoned house foundations and taro patches and then, higher up, rows upon rows of ditched garden beds and mounds (see map 2). Similar evidence of extensive resource exploitation can be found in the lagoon, where there are numerous stone fish traps, only some of which have been kept in good repair. A land census done in Dalipebinaw (an economically representative, though rather small, municipality of

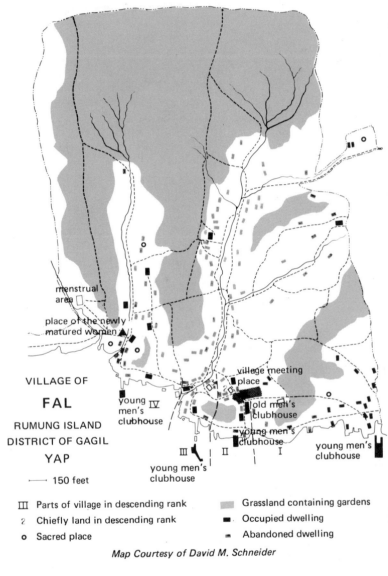

menstrual
area

place of the newly
matured women

VILLAGE OF

FAL

RUMUNG ISLAND
DISTRICT OF GAGIL
YAP

⟶ 150 feet

village meeting
place

young
men's
clubhouse

IV

old men's
clubhouse

young men's
clubhouse

young men's
clubhouse

III

II

I

young men's
clubhouse

III	Parts of village in descending rank		Grassland containing gardens
2	Chiefly land in descending rank	■	Occupied dwelling
o	Sacred place	▬	Abandoned dwelling

Map Courtesy of David M. Schneider

Map 2. Map of Fal village showing abandoned house plots

eight villages) found that attached to the 158 residential units which were surveyed there were 2,689 taro patches, 2,127 gardens, and 177 stone fish trap sites; only 20 percent of the taro patches and 6 percent of the garden plots were in use in 1951 at the time of the census (Mahoney 1958).

The overwhelming impression one gets from these figures, as well as from simple observation, is that traditional Yap had reached an extremely high level of development of subsistence resources. The people of Yap were no longer the introducers of culture, reducing the wilds to order, nor was the land an unworked resource, undeveloped and natural. The Yapese worked land and sea resources whose productivity had been extensively developed; they maintained and perhaps improved the taro patches, the fish traps, and the gardens that had already been built. Not surprisingly, it is with this fact that traditional Yapese ideology was fundamentally concerned.

Basic to Yapese social organization were the *ganong*, or "clan," and the *tabinaw,* or "landed estate." There were thirty to forty clans on Yap, each clan including persons from all over the island, of all ranks and statuses. Clan membership was a fact of birth, a child belonging to its mother's clan and tracing its descent through women from one original ancestress. Clan membership formed a basic part of a person's social identity and indicated which historical group he or she was a part of. There were no set relations among clans other than their exogamy, any clan marrying into and taking women from any other, nor did there appear to be any preferences as to which clans should intermarry.

While everyone belonged to one or another of the clans, all land on Yap belonged to one or another *tabinaw* estate. The stable core of the estate was a plot of land upon which had been built a raised stone foundation (*dayif*) and a house where a man and his wife and children would live. To this central nucleus were attached the garden land, taro patches, fishing area, and other resources owned by the *tabinaw*. Depending on its location and rank, an estate could include portions of the lagoon area and of mangrove swamps, forest land, freshwater streams, and sections of the high grassy inland area, as well as plots on which paths, public buildings, and meeting areas were built within the village.

The *tabinaw*, however, supplied more than just subsistence and living space to its occupants. It also was a source of social status. People on Yap held whatever status and authority their land conferred upon them. To the Yapese, people did not simply act on their own, expressing themselves; rather, they expressed those roles that were seen to reside within their land. That is, a man was chief specifically because he held chief's land; a magician, because he held magician's land. People are not chief, it was said; the land is chief. Those who commanded and those who obeyed were cast in either role by the land they held. Those who were without land, having been disinherited or forced from it, had no voice in social affairs and, in an important sense, had ceased to be a part of Yapese society.

A clan had no permanent claims to land, nor any inherent status. Whereas a man stayed on his natal estate to represent the status it held, his sister married out and, following the rule of clan exogamy, established herself on the estate held by a man of a different clan. Since it was her children and not those of her brother who would have membership in their clan, their own clan descendants would come to live on a different estate (that of the wife's husband) from the one they had been born upon, while their own natal estate would pass to a different clan, that of the brother's wife.

A woman was said to be like the navigator (*puluw*) of a canoe who looks for a place to stop. The future of the clan lay with her. If she guided the canoe to a lower, inconsequential estate, it was not good. If she found an estate of the same rank as the one she left, it was acceptable. But if she guided the canoe to a higher estate, it was good indeed. A man was like the stone mooring post (*wag*) put near the shore to tie up canoes. He stayed in the same place, never moving, but accepting on his estate a woman who came from another clan. Through the women who married off the estate each generation, the people of the clans thus moved from estate to estate, successively claiming different land and taking different statuses, while at the same time the estate itself was passed from clan to clan, as is shown in figure 1. It was out of the simultaneous movement of clan and estate that the Yapese conceived the social order to be generated and to persist, structuring not only the relations between people but also the most fundamental relations of land and people, nature and culture. This becomes clear in the more specific ideology of clan and estate.

The estate on Yap was conceptualized as a distinct and continuous unit of land imbued with its own particular social powers. It was seen to have been sectioned off from a larger unit of land as men had passed it on to their sons. While the eldest son would inherit his father's house and authority, younger sons would be given plots carved out of the father's estate on which they could build new house foundations and houses and start new estates. The father could even give some of the statuses held by the original estate to those just being created; not the major ones, of course, but something to give the new estate at least some social significance. The rock foundation of the father's land would be called the *kengin e dayif*, the "trunk foundation," the others being thought to branch treelike from it. As such subdivision of the estate took place, each estate became the "trunk," *kengin e dayif* to those sectioned from it and, at the same time, had its own "trunk" elsewhere. If a father had inherited other estates because there had been no closer heirs to receive them, he would also parcel them out to his sons. Under the increasing population at the time of the traditional culture, however, estate subdivision was probably more likely. If the land ran out altogether, I was told, a younger son might ask his father where his land was. The father would point to the basket used to collect coconut husks for making coconut fiber rope (*lib ko aw*). The son was expected to make rope that he could exchange for shell or stone money and then buy land.

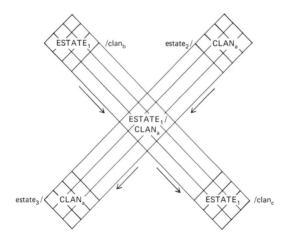

Fig. 1. The movement of the clan and the estate

Although all people were by birth alone members of clans, this, we saw, gave them no particular status or claim to land from which they could make a living. It was only by gaining membership in an estate, through the movement of the clan women, that people came to have their particular social identities and claims to land.

Each estate itself had a name and carried a set of ancestral names that would be given to the children born on it. The names (*ngacal*) referred to ancestors who had lived and worked on the land and who were seen to remain there after death as spirits, the *thigith*. To have a name from a given estate gave a man a claim on its land and the statuses with which it was imbued. People explained the term *ngacal*, "land name," by associating it with *ngucol*, the three stones used to form a tripod to hold a cooking pot over a fire. If you had no name, they said, you had no land and no place to put your cooking pot, no place from which to eat. Just as the three rocks (*ngucol*) support a pot, so the name (*ngacal*) that gave a person his land supported him. Without the three-rock tripod, a man's cooking pot was nearly useless; without a name and land, so was he. Although a woman took her name from the pool of ancestral spirits of the estate in which she was born, this did not entitle her to land. Rather, it identified her with a woman who had married into that estate, borne children there, and died, becoming one of its spirits. The girl would do likewise, marrying out to another estate where, upon her death, she would become one of its spirits.

People were not only named for their predecessors on the estate, however. More important, they were also seen to represent them socially. Each estate contained a "voice" (*lungun*) for which its occupants "spoke" in social affairs. It was this voice that defined their social position. A man was chief because he spoke for land which had a chief's voice; a magician, because he spoke for land with a magician's voice. The voice itself was that of the previous land-holders. To speak for the land was to speak for one's father and, ultimately, for the general pool of ancestral spirits.

The importance of the ancestors on the land, it was explained, was that it was they who had made the land what it was, had developed its resources, built its gardens, its taro patches, and its fishing equipment, and it was they who had earned for it the social position that its occupants represented. Even though it was generally not remembered how a given estate came to have its particular voice or social position, there was no question that it had been a result of the efforts of the ancestors. The ancestors who had lived and worked on the land before were seen to have incorporated themselves into it by their labor. Just as the labor they invested to maintain and develop the estate's physical and social resources remained, so they themselves remained on the estate as spirits, living in the rock foundations of its dwellings and providing it with a voice. People were named for and spoke for their predecessors on the estate because they benefited from the labor those predecessors had invested—labor that, in transforming and defining the land, transformed and defined the people who now came to live from it.

The concept of invested labor or effort, of *magar*, was pervasive in Yapese culture. It was a concept that acknowledged the work done on someone's behalf, the energy that had been expended. To thank a person was to say, "*kum magar*," "you are tired," "you have done something on my behalf." That the concept was given such emphasis with respect to the estate was due particularly to the fact that the estate, as we have seen, was not continuously held by one clan, but was passed from group to group. The transmission of the estate was more accurately a transaction of the estate, a transfer of title between clans in return for appropriate payment.

Each successive woman who came to the estate and bore children belonged to a different clan from the previous woman and her children—that is, the husband's mother, the husband himself, and his siblings. This was insured by the rule of clan exogamy. The woman and her children themselves formed a distinct clan group, a different "people" unrelated to the clan group who held the land. Having no prior rights to the estate, they could take possession of it only as they repaid equal value to the preceding group. This was reflected in all the relations of the estate—the relations of mother and child, who belonged to the same clan, being based on mutuality and sharing; the relations of husband and wife or father and child, who belonged to different clans, being based on exchange and reciprocity.

Marrying in, a woman was said to "hook the land" (*l'eg e binaw*) as one would hook a fish. In paying for it, she was said to "cut the bones out of the land" (*thab i yil' e binaw*) or to "cut the bones out of the work invested" (*thab i yil' e magar*). Just as one would cut the bones out of a fish before eating it, it was explained, so a woman had to remove that which obstructed her clear title to the estate; specifically, the preceding group's claim to it. To do so she had to fulfill two obligations to them: in exchange for the land itself she had to produce the children who could be the preceding group's heirs on the estate, their own clan descendants having been established elsewhere with the marriage of the husband's sister; and, equally important, to repay the *magar,* or invested labor, of the husband's clan group, she and the children she bore had to work for them on the estate. One extremely precise older person differentiated between "cutting the bones out of the land" and "cutting the bones out of the work invested" on this basis. The former, he said, was fulfilled in the exchange of children for land; the latter, in the exchange of labor for labor.

The exchange of children for land took place as a woman became pregnant on the man's estate and bore children; she could not bring children with her if she had been previously married and divorced. If a woman produced no children, or bore fewer children than were desired, then the exchange could be accomplished through adoption (*pof*). The preferred adoption was for a woman to receive a child from her own close clan sisters so that the exchange relations between clan groups would be maintained and the proceeds of the woman's labors would still go to her own clan group. It was considered least desirable to take a child from the man's clan relatives.

The repayment of labor between clan groups took place as one group reenacted or reproduced what the previous group had already done on the land. A man's wife, it was said, was like his mother. When an emissary from the man's estate went to a woman's father to ask for the woman in marriage, he would not say that the man wanted to take her for a wife, but rather that he wanted to "make her a mother" (*citiningiy*). The woman would be made a mother both in the sense that she would bear children to whom the estate would in turn be passed, and in the sense that she would take the place of the man's mother, caring and providing for him by working on the estate as she had worked. The woman had to work her husband's land, planting his gardens and maintaining his taro patches, harvesting his food, taking care of the internal domestic affairs of the estate, caring for the children, and helping in the care of his aging parents, all the while putting up with his abuses and weaknesses and providing him with support.

As the people of the estate generally respected the ancestral spirits who had held and worked the land before them, so the woman and her children were to respect the man as a "sacred object" (*banoth*), to be dutifully honored and obeyed. In that the children were hers, belonging to her clan, the woman was responsible to see that they showed the appropriate respect to their father; in this sense, she acted as their "navigator" (*puluw*) by guiding them toward the behavior that would insure their claim to the land.

The child was required to repay the labor expended on its behalf, particularly that of its father. Father and child were said to "exchange care" (*thil e chugol*) on the estate. The father would provide for the child when it was young and incapable of looking after itself, and then the child, when it had grown up, would provide and care for its father as he grew old and incapable of looking after himself, a son bringing fish to his father as his father had provided fish for him, and so on. A "child" (*fak*) was preeminently someone who had to be cared for. The term as well as the related verb form *fakay* ("to take possession of," "adopt"), could be applied to anything living that a person came to possess—dogs, chickens, pigs, or people—anything depending upon its "owner" for its existence. People pointed out that when a man became old and helpless and needed to be cared for, he was in a position analogous to that of his child when it was young. When a father became old and helpless he addressed his sons as *tam*, short for *citamangin* ("father"), and his daughters as *tin,* short for *citiningin* ("mother"),[1] being like a "child" to them. To return a father's care was also to "cut the bones out of the work invested," for it repaid the father for his labor on behalf of the children, leaving them with clear title to the land. If an aging father was ignored by his children, he was perfectly within his rights to pass the land on to whomever came to take care of him as he grew old.

It was in this context also that the son would come to represent his father in social affairs. Although many basic skills such as swimming, fishing, or canoeing could be learned from slightly older age-mates or siblings and much general lore could be absorbed from the discussion of older men at the men's houses and community centers, it was only as the son helped and obeyed his father that he would be taught the skills and knowledge specifically associated with the estate—the intricacies of its political position or its technical or ritual expertise—and given responsibility for "speaking" for it. This process would begin almost as soon as the son was able to walk, the father at first directing the child in the simplest tasks, such as carrying a betel nut to another person or fetching a tool, but gradually assuming a more and more distant and aloof position as a respected authority with whom one could not speak jokingly or crudely, leaving his son to seek him out on his own initiative and earn from him the estate knowledge and the exercise of its prerogatives. As the son grew in his knowledge, the father would delegate more and more authority to him as he himself became too old to move about, the son thus coming to "speak" for his father.

Each successive clan group worked to repay the labors of those who had come before, from whom they received the estate, and they were repaid in turn by the labors of those who came after, to whom they passed the estate. Consequently, when a man required his son to act as his father had, he equated the two men both in the roles they performed and also in name. Ideally, men's names alternated on the estate (e.g., Wa'ath—Ken—Wa'ath—Ken), each man naming his eldest son, the one who would take his place on the land, after his father. This equation of grandfather and first son in a sense guaranteed the continuity of the land's "voice" and that each clan group would receive what had been demanded of it.

As the estate was transacted from one group to another, then, it was defined ideologically not simply as land but as land that contained a critical investment of labor—labor on which the people had come to depend, both socially and personally. The ideology, in effect, described the estate in terms of the fundamental social realities that defined the land of Yap itself—the way people lived from it, worked it, invested themselves in it, and passed it on to the next generation. To the Yapese, in sum, the estate *was the land* taken as an objective entity, the productive resource that supported the people on the basis of its own particular history of development.

Just as the estate was the land of Yap, so the clans were the people. The clan was described simply as a group of people historically derived from a common source, "one branching tree of people" (*tab kae' girdi*). It was seen to have begun at a specific estate, the "base" or "trunk" (*tabulbul/tana'aen e ganong*) of the clan, and to have branched out from there, moving from estate to estate. The clan was conceptualized less as a solidary group than as a developmental line. Although people did not distinguish any subsections of the clan as groups, they did distinguish the place from which their particular line of the clan was remembered to have come. The estate as far back as could be remembered from which a woman's mother's mother's ... mother had come was their "root," their *likegal'*—their hibiscus tree root. Hibiscus trees grow by dropping their roots from their branches; where one takes root in the ground, a new tree grows. While almost everything else that grew onto people's land belonged to them, a hibiscus tree which grew over onto their land from their neighbor's still belonged to the neighbor who owned the parent tree.[2] In a similar way, people said, women married out of the estate, taking root and bearing children elsewhere, but still belonged to the original tree from which they came.

The legends of clan origins generally represent the clans as beginning with a woman who appeared on Yap, married into a particular estate, and bore children who would carry on her line. The origin stories themselves were not well remembered, perhaps because the particular manner of origin of any specific clan was not significant to its structure or its relations with other clans. But the very incomplete information we do have is suggestive. The stories appear to interpret from various perspectives the basic episode of clan survival, the process of incorporation by which a newly emerged branch of the clan was taken into Yapese society with each generation.

One group of stories relates how a newborn girl child was found under a plant or beside an animal that was assumed to have given birth to it, to be its mother. The child would be taken into an estate, would grow up, marry, and have children, establishing a new clan of people descended from the plant or animal. The plant or animal would thereafter be honored as the founder of the clan, not to be eaten, killed, or otherwise harmed by members of that clan.

The natural objects indicated as the mothers of such children were remarkable in that they consistently were things that lived a parasitic or scavenger's existence: a small crab (*li'l*) and rat (*bro'*) that scavenge off rotten things and human refuse; a fungus (*porfiy*) that grows on dead wood; a species of yam (*dol*) that grows wild without cultivation. People would explain these stories to me by saying that the child really had been abandoned by its human mother, perhaps because she already had too many children at home. But this explanation only served to underline what appears to be the basic point of the stories—that a clan was produced when a woman who had no land, and was thus abandoned, came to the estate, participated in it as a wife, and bore children. This, of course, reflected the pattern of their lives. The women of the clan were required to move off their natal estates and therefore had no land themselves. They were landless, abandoned, like scavengers living off others. The clan itself was reproduced each generation only as these landless women came to marry onto an estate and bore their children on it. We might include as a subgroup of this category the few stories that recount essentially the same episode but tell of a girl who was washed up on Yap from another land. This is landlessness in another sense, but it seems to make the same point: that the clan was produced when a woman with no land to work joined in the productive relations of the estate.

Other origin stories appear to look at the process of the clan from the perspective of the clan's transformational effect on the estate. In these stories, instead of a natural child being rescued and brought into culture, a woman spirit (*kan*) or her child is trapped on Yap and taken into an estate where she marries and has children. Of course, it was not simply that the people were transformed by being taken onto the land; the land, too, was transformed by taking on people who would work it and give it value. Thus, here the originator of the clan is a spirit, preeminently a cultural being, who is caught by the estate. It is tempting to try to account for this change in perspective by noting that several stories of clans started by a spirit-woman also involved particularly high-ranking estates (Fanif clan at Arib; Weloy clan at Buluwol; and perhaps even Ngolog clan at Ru'uway), but data are lacking.

Perhaps the best-known story is that of the porpoise clan (Gucig), which significantly brings together both themes. A spirit who took the form of a porpoise came to see a dance on Yap from her home on Sipin, a nearby island known to be inhabited by spirits. On landing, she took off her porpoise tail and buried it near a coconut tree. A man discovered the tail and hid it. When the spirit came back after the dance, she could not find her tail and thus could not return home. The man found her crying under the tree and offered to take her back to his home, where she might live, not telling her that he had found her porpoise tail and hidden it. They married and had children. Eventually the spirit woman found the porpoise tail where the man had hidden it and, leaving her children, returned to her own land. Her children and their descendants began the porpoise clan.

Here the foundress of the clan was both a spirit and an animal— an animal who shed her animal qualities and married into the estate. Furthermore, it is the human qualities of the animal that seem to be significant here, rather than the natural qualities of the person as in the plant/animal children stories. People described the porpoise as quasi-human: the animal would come up to a canoe and speak to it, indicating it wanted to race; when caught and brought on shore, it would cry with a voice like that of a person. In this story, it appears, the clan is seen in its dual role as the people who were produced when a woman was taken onto the land, giving up her natural or animal identity, and also as the cultural beings, the "spirits," who came to live and work on the land.

The clans generally had no organized structure of power, nor did they act as groups. To some extent the people of the same clan held their land in common. They were said to be able to ask for things belonging to each other's land without considering repayment—this on the grounds that they were sharing what "their" land provided. In practicality, however, the lack of any general clan organization and the fact that people of the same clan could be of widely divergent ranks and statuses, and therefore bound by very strong patterns of authority and deference, limited this "sharing" to those who also maintained relations on other grounds, either as close kin or as friends.

The clans were seen to be merely the human resource that produced the people who lived and worked on the estates. This is made quite clear in the Yapese notion of human reproduction. A woman was said to be a "garden" (*milay'*) that the man planted by introducing the seed that grew into the plant that was the child. The man was the laborer who "worked on" (*marwelnag*) the woman. One person explained that the feeling a man had in orgasm was due to the fact that the strength from all the blood vessels in his body went into the sperm and the work of implanting it in the woman. It was further said that if a man engaged in too much sex, he would become exhausted, weak, and depleted, having given up all his strength. A woman, on the other hand, would not become worn out by sex itself but only by bearing many children—an exhaustion that, incidentally, was thought to be more becoming than that resulting from a man's overindulgence. A man, as "laborer," would wear himself out by "laboring"; a woman, as "garden" or "land," by depleting her natural productivity. The ancestral ghosts (*thigith*) played an important role in this process, too, making the man's "work" on the woman's "land" productive by facilitating the conception and development of the child if they were pleased with what they saw on the estate and by rendering it unproductive and sterile if they were not—much as they would oversee the productive work on the estate generally.

While a woman came to a man's land and worked on it, planting his gardens, so a man "worked" on the woman's "land," planting it. People frequently put the relation of man and woman exactly in those terms. One person associated the words *milay'* ("garden") and *malae'* ("marriage"). *Milay'* means a place where one digs (*lay'*) in the ground with a digging stick to plant crops. This was what a woman did on her husband's land as she worked to possess it and what it produced. When a woman married (*ke un ko malae'*), he said, she became her husband's garden (*milay'*), which he "worked" on in a similar fashion as he took possession of her and what she produced.

Because the father planted the seed, the child was definitely related to him. To ask who a person's father was, one could ask whose "blood" he was, although this was a bit delicate, as it was essentially asking who had implanted the child in the mother. Although it was difficult for a father to disinherit his child, the product of his seed and labor, because he would be "throwing away his blood," the child did not belong to him or his clan. The child explicitly belonged to the mother and her clan. The mother was the "garden," the "land" out of which the child grew. The child belonged to the mother and her clan as one product of a specific natural fertility that had originated with the clan's founding ancestress and now continued through the women of the clan, producing children as different men "worked" upon them. Likewise, the people of the clans were seen to be grouped together because they had emerged from the same human natural resource, the same "land."

Just as the resources of the estate could be developed, so could the resources of the clan. Although the women who would bear the next generation of the clan would neither "speak" for nor remain on the land on which they were born, that land still determined their status in the village rank system and thereby broadly determined the status of the estate into which they could marry. As we shall see in detail in chapter 5, village rank was extremely important in Yapese life. People of lower rank were considered more "dirty" or "polluting" (taay) than people of higher rank, less socially developed, and consequently limited in their sphere of social action. They could not go into certain areas of the village or into certain taro patches, and they had to show deference to those of higher rank. As a clan worked to claim a succession of higher and higher estates, however, it could develop itself socially, allowing each following generation greater rank and power. It was because of this that a woman was expected to marry onto land that was at least equal in rank to her natal estate, at least maintaining the level of development that the resources of the clan had attained. She was definitely not to marry onto lower land. That would be to demean herself as well as to waste the labor that had gone into establishing the position her mother had already achieved for her clan at her natal estate.

The clans, then, were defined ideologically as continuous lines of people having, like the estates, their own particular histories of development. Where the ideology presented the estate as the land of

Yap, here it presented the clans as the people of Yap. The clans were the human reproductive resource, the people who sustained the Yapese way of life as they moved from estate to estate. They were the people as they both lived from the developed productivity of the land and created and perpetuated that productivity. The movement of the estate and the clan, their double treelike growth, thus involved the social evolution of land and people, the two most basic resources of Yapese culture.

Although the estate and the clan each had a continuity of its own, it should be clear from what has been said so far that the two were fundamentally dependent on each other. The estate was seen to continue to produce only as the people came to it anew each generation and reenacted in their own lives the patterns of action those before them had enacted, doing the tasks they had done, speaking the "voice" they had spoken. If the land were not worked, its gardens not kept up and replanted, or if its prerogatives were not exercised, then, it was claimed, the labor that had gone into it previously would lose its value.

There was a sense, too, in which maintaining the developed productivity of the estate depended specifically on clanspeople who were developed to at least a nearly commensurate level. A woman from an extremely low estate could not establish herself on a high estate because, being considered low and polluting, she and her family would not be able to engage in the marriage exchanges of food and valuables that would establish her on the land, nor might she be able to perform her duties as wife, perhaps even being prohibited from entering her husband's gardens and cooking his food. For the productivity of the land of the estate to be at least maintained, both physically and socially, the people of the clans had to be reproduced on it also, both physically and socially.

Reciprocally, the continuing reproduction of the people of the clans depended upon the process of production from the land. The clans continued to reproduce physically and socially only as they gained an estate that could support them and give them a "voice." To maintain whatever power and authority their clan line had achieved, the people thus had to find an estate productive enough to maintain them as their forebears had been maintained, an estate at least commensurate with their own status.

This interdependence between clan and estate was stated by the ideological constructs we have been examining. The ideology of speaking for the voice of the land explicitly characterized the continuity of the developed productivity of the land in terms of a continuing human quality, a voice. It defined the coninuing productivity of the land specifically in terms of the qualities of the people who would live and work on it. In so doing, it stated in very exact terms that production from the land was a process of reproducing the people. Similarly, the ideology of the clans characterized the continuity of the people in terms of land. As we have seen, the reproduction of the clan was said to involve a form of gardening in which the man "worked" on the woman's "land" to produce children, the clan continuing as land was made to produce. This stated in equally exact terms that the reproduction of people was a process of producing from the land. The attributes of the people had come to be the attributes of the land, and the attributes of the land had come to be those of the people. The ideology of clan and estate articulated a fundamental dialectic of survival on Yap in which it was the productivity of the land that determined the productivity of the people on it and, at the same time, the productivity of the people that determined the productivity of their land.

The interaction of the clan and the estate, of course, took place most concretely in the marriage of man and woman. As a woman and her clan needed what a man's land produced, subsistence and social status, so a man and his land needed what a woman produced, children who would work to maintain the value of his land. The two were seen as complementary. While a man's land was that on which he was born, a woman was said to "have her land in her legs" (*ba tafen u ay*). This referred not only to the fact that she had to move out and establish herself elsewhere from where she was born, but also to the fact that she herself was seen as the "land," the "garden," that produced children. Although a woman was landless in one sense, she did have a kind of "land"—her reproductivity—that she could exchange for the land a man held. The labor that we have seen to be exchanged in the transaction of land fit within this pattern also. Just as the land provided by a man to support and maintain the woman's clan group was exchanged for the children she bore to continue the man's estate, so the labor he specifically contributed for their support was exchanged for the labor they provided to maintain his estate.

It was in the context of this exchange that a child came to be a member of an estate. The exchange itself would begin in the love affairs conducted secretly at night outside the village. One of the main enjoyments of Yapese life—as recounted in countless songs of loves desired, won, lost, betrayed, rendered impossible, and so on—

was the secret romantic involvements both before and after marriage, either as casual affairs or as long-term relationships. Love affairs were the main preoccupation of the young, who were allowed a great deal of sexual freedom, though they were certainly not confined to young people. If, as the result of an affair, a man brought a woman home to live with him, publicly acknowledging the relationship, and the arrangement was sanctioned by the couple's parents, they were thereafter considered married. The children that the woman produced then would belong to the man's estate as the product of the reproductive "land" he had come to possess. Once they had been named with the names of the man's estate, the children would not leave that land even if their mother divorced (*cuw*) and returned to her natal estate, a not infrequent occurrence. Very small dependent children might accompany their mother upon divorce, but when they had reached the age of four or five they were to be returned to the father, who was to have helped provide for them in the meantime.

Not all love affairs would, or could, lead to marriage. Because the production of children was an important part of the marriage exchange, the child of an adulterous union or the child of an unmarried woman was called "the child of a thief" (*fak e morowrow*), a very strong epithet. Both the woman and her lover were "thieves," having stolen that which belonged as part of the exchange between husband and wife: the man stealing another man's "land," the woman stealing another woman's means of claiming her husband's land. The child of an unmarried woman (*fak e mucugubil*—the phrase itself further being a derogatory epithet) was also in a very precarious position, having no land that it was rightfully entitled to live on by birth.

All of daily life was seen to revolve around the cooperation and exchange centered on the estate through marriage; it was the result of contributions of both the man and the woman. A man and a woman were said to be like the two halves of a palm frond (*yuw*), fitting together at all points to make a unity. A woman was to provide food from the gardens (*gagan*) and stay at the estate to take care of domestic affairs. A man was to provide fish or seafood (*thumag*), going fishing alone or with other men of the village. No meal was thought complete without both food from the gardens and food from the sea. A man was also responsible for providing a house for his family and for representing his estate in village works and external affairs. While a woman stayed at home, a man moved about in social and political concerns. A woman was thought to be the base and support of the estate; she was compared to the hull of a canoe (*bulel*), carrying and holding all. The man, moving about and taking with him the "voice" of the estate, was thought to be the mast (*wolyang*) on the canoe, providing it with the means to move about in social affairs. Both were important, but the woman was somehow more fundamental. If the woman of the house died, the people in it were in severe difficulty: "their canoe had split" (*ke pil e m'uwrorad*). Without the woman, the hull, what good was the man, the mast? On what could it rest? Yet without the mast, the estate's effectiveness and importance were gone, too. Both were necessary, as it was only by their different labors that the estate was a cohesive and functioning whole.

The exchange betwen man and woman was thus fundamental to Yapese life. Through it people came to be born on the land, to work it as it had been worked before them, and to bring about the birth of those who would work it after them. Through it, the land and people defined and transformed each other, the man being the means by which a woman's clan was perpetuated, the "laborer" on her "land," and the woman and her children being the means by which the man's estate was perpetuated and developed, the laborers on his land. The exchange was at once the interaction of the people and the land, of the reproductive relations of the clan and the productive relations of the estate, and of man and woman. We can thus diagram as in figure 2.

It was *only* through the proper execution of this exchange that the perpetuation of Yapese life was conceived to be possible. This was made quite clear by the prohibition of marriage and all sexual relations between kinsmen, either of the same estate or of the same clan.

All those who were seen to retain a claim on the estate as it was passed from father to son were considered kinsmen, as we shall see in detail later. Any sexual relations, and certainly marriage, within this group was classified as incest (*k'uw*) and was said to offend the ancestral ghosts of the estate, who would retaliate against the offenders by bringing disease, accident, or serious misfortune upon them.

This seems to follow from the dynamics we have already established. Since sexual relations figured centrally in the exchange between man and woman that resulted in the passage of land from father to son, for a man to offer his sexual "labors" or a woman her sexual "land" was to initiate the process of that exchange. Those of the estate group all had claims on the land based on the labor which either they or someone related to them through the proper ties of kinship had invested in the land; so it was clearly undesirable to attempt this exchange among themselves. The people who had worked the land would only receive a return on their labor as others came to earn the land from them. It would thus be unproductive to take onto the land those who already had a claim to it and who would not need to work fully to earn it, to maintain the level of productivity it had reached. Incest within the estate group appears to have threatened the process by which the labor invested in the land was maintained and enhanced over the generations. Hence it was appropriate that the ancestral spirits should be the ones to retaliate against a union that lessened their own importance and all they had worked for.

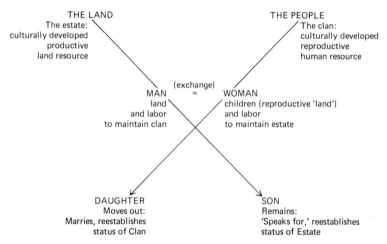

Fig. 2. The ideology of the movement of clan and estate

Similarly, the continuation of the clan was seen as depending on the rule of exogamy. Any incest within the clan was said to result in the extinction of that particular clan. People were not exactly sure how or when it would "die out" (*math e mit*), but it was felt generally that the women of the clan would cease to become pregnant or would bear only sickly or weak children.

This again appears to fit with the analysis already presented. In that the people of the clan were seen to be grouped together as the products of the same human fertility, of the same "land" or of the same nature, it appears that this prohibition of sexual relations within the clan meant at the most general level that those of one nature could not reproduce and persist of themselves. Incest within the clan would be an attempt to produce from the "land," from nature alone, without its being labored upon. It follows that anything that would grow from this attempt would have, in a sense, grown wild—would lack the transforming input of culture and might be sickly or weak. The clans were a human natural resource that, like the land, had come to be productive only as they were worked upon culturally.

More specifically, the prohibition seems to reflect the same kind of logic as the prohibition of sexual relations within the estate group. Since members of the same clan were already seen to share their land, they would not need to earn the land from one another. And if the people did not work to earn the land, not only would it lose value, but so would they, their own status being linked directly to the labor invested in the land. The statement that incest within the clan would lead to its extinction appears to mean that since sexual relations could initiate an exchange that could diminish the cultural value of the land and the people, incest could indeed lead to their eventual "extinction." The ideology of clan and estate, in effect, not only stated what must be done for the people and the land to survive and prosper together, but also warned what must not be done lest that survival be seriously threatened.

Thus far we have been able to see that Yapese ideology articulated in its own terms an analysis of what had come to be the condition of social life on Yap. It presented Yapese culture as operating simultaneously in two dimensions, being essentially the product of their interrelation. On the one hand, the people, genetically continuous in the clan, gave up one piece of land and took another. On the other hand, the land, holding a continuous social identity, gave up one group of people, those of one clan, and took another, those of another clan. The people exchanged land, and the land exchanged people. Yapese culture was created and perpetuated through these two processes, the first defining the people and the second defining the land.

Both resources, we saw, had been defined by a history of development. Life on Yap, the relations of land and people, had become more complex than a simple dialectic between nature and culture, between the labor that the people culturally invested in planting the land to exploit its natural fertility and the natural fertility of the land that made the people's labor productive. On Yap, the land had come to produce for the people not of its natural fertility alone, but as that fertility had been developed by the labor invested in it—as it had taken on the cultural attributes of the people. It had become at once a natural resource developed by culture and a cultural resource, a repository of labor, that developed the natural resources of the people, their natural reproductivity, and their own natural abilities to act in society.

The people likewise had come to produce from the land not simply as they worked it and culturally transformed it themselves, but as they worked on the basis of the labor that had previously developed the land, as they became the natural resource that allowed the cultural investment in the land to be productive. The people had come to be at once the cultural beings who transformed the land and the natural beings who were transformed by the cultural investment already in it; and the land had come to be at once the natural object transformed by the people's cultural labors and the cultural object that transformed them. Yapese culture was perceived ideologically as the people and the land bound together in their mutual develop- ✓ ment, a dialectic involving the clans who came to transform the land and the estates that transformed the people—the people as they continually adapted and readapted to the land, and the land as it continually adapted and readapted to the people.

To say this is of course to generalize the broadest possible meaning from the ideology, to take it as a statement about social reality in the most abstracted form. But having abstracted this dialectic, we can now begin to recognize it in the actual process of Yapese history, operating at the level of the forms of clan and estate themselves.

The interaction of clan and estate appears to be at base a historical interaction. The internal logic of the ideology we have been discussing seems to indicate that the clans had an existence before the estates; that they were prior historical forms in terms of which the estates were created. People were seen to live from the labor of their ancestors on the estates specifically as those ancestors were already defined as members of different clans. It was the estate members' different clan affiliations that shaped the relations between them and formed the rationale for the transaction of land and labor. Clan relations, in other words, appear logically to be the point of departure for estate relations. That people "spoke" for the "voice" of the *land* itself also seems to reflect that they lived expressly from the estate itself, not as they were identified with a particular corporate group that owned it and worked it but rather as they were seen to be but one in a succession of different established groups who had come to that estate, worked it, and passed it on.

Although it is impossible to know the precise history of Yapese society, it seems safe to assume that the clans did exist before the formation of the estates, as the logic of estate relations suggests. Comparative evidence does show that corporate matrilineal clan groups were widespread through the Carolines, indeed called by terms cognate with the Yapese *ganong*. Virtually all the island societies surrounding Yap were characterized by matrilineal descent groups, but none evidenced a form of organization identical to the Yapese estate. The clans on Yap could thus well have been existing matrilineal groups similar to those found elsewhere in Micronesia[3] that were forced to adapt themselves to the particular changing conditions on Yap. As it appears to have been the social relationship of the clan that defined the productive relations of the estate, so clan relations could have come in turn to be defined by those of the estates. As all authority came to reside with the men of the estates, the once-corporate clans could have been redefined simply as a historical reproductive group, without organization or power, whose main significance was that it contained women, the natural resource that produced the men who would speak for the land.

It is only when they are looked at in this manner, we should note, that the relations between clan and estate begin to emerge as truly *dialectical*. For as estate relations appear both to arise out of and to oppose (negate) clan relations historically, the relation of clan and estate becomes more than simply a "balanced interaction" between mutually defining and effecting terms. Rather, clan and estate take on the sense of being the contradictory and antagonistic terms of a historical process, a process that through contradiction and antagonism possesses its own immanent direction, its own future as well as its own past.

After our description of Yapese culture becomes more complete, we will be able to try to outline the general conditions that led to the establishment of the estate and the redefinition of the clan. It is enough now, however, simply to identify the clan as a historical form adapted to new material necessities and the estate as an organization of productive forces adapted from existing social forms. This in itself is significant, because it indicates that the interaction of clan and estate was from the beginning an interaction of the people and their history with the land and the concrete material conditions under which they found it possible to live. It indicates that the ideology itself was, in effect, a construct of Yapese history, a set of inter-related categories defined by and within that history.

3 "Our Land Belongs to Someone Else; Someone Else's Land Belongs to Us"

The dialectical interaction of people and land, clan and estate shaped not only the relations of the people within a particular estate, but also the relations of the people of different estates. The estate itself was seen to consist not only of the domestic group living on specific land, but also of an entire extended network of relations of people and land. The term *tabinaw* was applicable to both domestic and extended groups, the one implying the other.

The establishment of broad networks of land and people resulted directly from the relations of clan and estate we have already described. Since the man's claim on his land began with his mother, who had worked to earn it for her children, the land was not simply his alone. It also belonged to his siblings, who were equally identified with the mother and who had similarly taken care of their father in his old age. Brothers, of course, would have been given pieces of their father's land, but sisters had to marry out. They could not stay to share in or profit from the land. Of this there was no question. For a woman to stay would imply that she would marry her brother, committing incest, which was considered a very strong offense. Brother-sister avoidance was strong. After puberty, they could not speak to each other directly or be alone together. They could not sleep in the same building, nor should a sister let the fragrance of her grass skirt blow downwind to her brother. Out-marrying sisters would take with them only a small piece of land, usually a taro patch or a garden, depending on the wealth of the estate. This land was called *gili'ungin,* a term that was glossed as meaning a place for the girl to put her grass skirt. It was thought of as a place from which she could eat were she to return to visit the estate, a symbol of her tie to it. But beyond this, a woman who married out took with her important rights in the estate she left.

Although the woman could not use the land she left at her natal estate, she and the children she bore stood as guardians to it, watching over those who had taken their place, the woman's brother's wife and her children. The woman and her children assumed this role as the continuation of her mother's people who had moved onto the land and worked to claim it with their labor. Even though they had moved from the land, they were to guard their people's investment in it, particularly as it was transacted to the succeeding generations. The woman and her children held the ultimate sanction of banishing the brother's wife and children from the land if, after the brother's death, it was seen that they abused their rights or did not fulfill their obligations. This role would pass through the clan line for four generations, to the woman's daughter's daughter's child. It was only after four generations had passed that the claim of the people established on the land by an in-marrying woman finally expired, that the clan group was fully repaid for its investment in the land. When there were no male heirs to an estate, as frequently occurred under depopulation, the woman and her children would themselves inherit the land, which could then be incorporated into the estate of the woman's husband. If there were neither male nor female heirs, the land would revert to the closest woman who had moved from the land in a previous generation, or to her children, who still might stand as its "guardian."

This line through the clan was called the *mafaen* of the estate, a woman and her children being *mafaen* over the next clan group who came to her natal estate. People explained the term *mafaen* in two ways. They associated it with the word *faen*, "owner," and said that the *mafaen* represented the established owners of the land, the people who had taken part in the work to earn it and who thus had a recognized claim on it. They also explained that the term, which is the word for a "generation" of people, meant exactly that: the *mafaen* represented the claim of one generation of people on the land, a claim that was passed on through the clan descendants, who could guard what their fellow clan members had worked for, making sure that what was owed was repaid.

A woman could not, of course, chase her brother's wife and children off the land without sufficient cause. People told of two types of *mafaen* who might attempt this: the "poor *mafaen*" (*mafaen ni gafugo*) who had married into a poor estate and wanted to recapture her lost wealth, and the "greedy *mafaen*" (*mafaen ni chugow*) who simply was out to get more land. Both would have been challenged by the brother's wife or children to show due cause for the eviction and asked, "What do you want that you take your land but you didn't just marry each other?" (*Mang e gimeth badag ni ngum tafenyeth tafenmeth mad dab mula'gath?*).

The *mafaen,* then, were the father's sister and her children, the people who had moved out to make way for a person's mother and him/herself. To them one owed the same respect one owed to one's father, for it was also their land. Though they had moved off, their claim to the land was prior, the same as the father's claim, being founded on the work of the father's mother. It was not simply the father who gave the land to his child. When a child was born to an estate, the *mafaen,* the father's sister, could be first to call out the child's name in the naming ceremony, the name that indicated the land the child would hold.

It was through these *mafaen* relations that each estate and each clan group was enmeshed in a wider social sphere. Because all clan groups retained *mafaen* rights, any specific clan group was at the center of a set of relations extending in two directions: on the one side to the estate from which a woman had originated and over which she and her children were *mafaen,* and on the other side to the estate onto which the woman who would become their *mafaen* had married (fig. 3). In establishing itself on an estate, the clan group

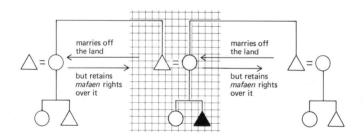

Fig. 3. *Mafaen* relations (solid lines connect clan members)

gave up the land it owned to be occupied and worked by others, and itself occupied and worked land others owned, thereby establishing at the same time relations with two other estates. This predicament · was stated in a saying that expressed the basic formula of Yapese land relations: *tafedad, tafen be; tafen be, tafedad*—"our land belongs to someone else; someone else's land belongs to us." One "people" remained the owner of the land another people had come to live on while those people remained the owners of the land they had left. That the estate and the clan generally depended on one another thus meant not only that the man and woman within the estate were dependent on one another, but also that the people of different estates depended on and were indebted to one another, earning the land from each other and guarding each other as *mafaen*.

It was precisely at the point of the transaction of land from one group to another, at marriages, that these interrelationships became most visible. In a series of three ceremonial exchanges between the people of the woman's estate and the people of the man's estate, the two groups fit the new claim on land established by the marriage into the series of claims and counterclaims made on the two estates —the claims stated in the "our land belongs to someone else ..." formula—and faced them off in a balanced exchange.

To perform such an exchange could involve the coordination of a great number of people, and the difficulty of doing this was noted by the general term used to designate it, *mitmit*. People explained the word, which referred both to the marriage exchanges and the larger intervillage exchanges, as meaning something like "repeatedly stuck" (*mit*—"stuck"). Problems and complications would always arise in such an event owing to the number of people involved, the perishability of the food exchanged, and the necessity of taking into account the tides both for fishing and for canoe travel. It had to work out that everyone could collect their food or fish at the same time, transport it to the place where the *mitmit* was to occur, and then return home with what they had received in exchange. Since this could involve hundreds of people, it was no small matter of logistics. To bring all the people together at once, to unravel the relations between them in the exchange, was perhaps difficult, but it was also an important demonstration of the viability of the basic formulations of Yapese society.

At the most general level, the marriage *mitmit* reflected the fact that the marriage was an exchange of the man's land as it had been developed by the labor his people had invested in it and the woman's labor power as it had been developed by the estate onto which her people had married and on which she was born. For this exchange to operate satisfactorily, there had to exist a parity between the people of the estate and the people marrying in. This is what the marriage exchanges were to establish. The resources of the people who held the estate had to be matched by the resources of the people who had come to earn it from them to show that the marriage was viable with respect to the interests of both parties involved.

The exchange was to work out symmetrically: for everything given, something was to be received; for everything received, something given. To repay something was to "kill it" (*li'*), to wipe it out so that nothing remained to be paid. Those on the woman's side were opposed to those on the man's side and, after the initial exchange, they competed to outgive each other—not to establish an imbalance, but to show that a balance really existed. The heads of the two estates would meet beforehand and discuss who was on each side so that no one would be left out or overlooked. In the actual exchange, those things given by either side were placed opposite each other in piles, physically demonstrating equivalence between the opposed sides. The two sides of the exchange were referred to as the two halves of a palm frond (*braba' e yuw nge braba'*). This was the same image used of a married couple, as we saw in chapter 2, referring here as it did there to the symmetrical opposition of the two sides in the exchange and its overall unity.

Even the marriage ceremony exchange between the estates mirrored the exchange between man and woman. The woman's side gave stone money (a woman's valuable) and that which a woman was responsible for, food from the gardens, while the man's side gave shell money (a man's valuable) and that which men were responsible for, fish, coconuts, and bananas. Stone money (*fae'*) was considered a woman's valuable because, outside the sexual allusion (stone money is a round, flat disk carried by sticking a pole through the hole in the middle),[1] it stays at the estate and does not go about in social affairs, like a woman. Shell money (*yar,* meaning "knife") was a man's valuable, both because of its phallic properties and because it was given more often and thereby moved around like a man.

The names of the three marriage *mitmit*s and some details differed within the various districts of Yap, but the basic pattern was the same everywhere. The description here is taken from Fanif municipality. There, the first *mitmit* was called *M'oy*. It was a small exchange and depended upon the distance between the estates of the two getting married for its comparative size: for those being married within the same village or close villages, it was only a token exchange involving a few goods, whereas for those from distant villages who had had few if any prior contact, it was more substantial. It rarely involved more than the immediate kinsmen of the man and woman. Still, it had the same fundamental form as the later and larger exchanges, and if we follow the path of the logic of the exchange, we can see generally how the marriage was fitted into the broader social context that surrounded it, how the larger structure of relations implicit in it was articulated and established.

Because the marriage itself involved the claims and counterclaims that different "peoples" had on an estate, the *M'oy* exchange concerned not only the man and the woman being married and their parents, but also the *mafaen* on both sides, the guardian-owners of the estates involved. The *mafaen* on the woman's side was her father's sister; on the man's side, his father's sister or, if married, his own sister. It was said that only a married woman could be a *mafaen* because only by marrying would she have land to give her "strength" in that role, to support her and her children as the guardians of her people's rights in her natal estate. In the *mitmit,* she was her brother's most significant support, his *gilay',* a term denoting the main corner beam of a house, or alternately his *yarif,* one who would help and work for him. It was specifically at the marriage *mitmit* that the *mafaen* were seen to "eat off" the land, to demand recognition of their claim to it. This did not mean that they ate what was produced by that land. Rather, it referred to the fact that the major portion of what was given to the estate was theirs. The *mafaen* contributed to the exchange to assert the claim of their people on the land and were paid back as the new claims of the other people were asserted in return.

To give was to establish or reaffirm a claim on the land or to counter another opposing claim. The coconuts, fish, and shell money that the man's side gave came mainly from his married sister or his father's sister. They would be the *mafaen* to the children of the woman who was marrying in, and everything they gave, as one man put it, said, "the land is mine, the land is mine." The garden food and stone money that the woman's side gave in return came mainly from her father's sister, the girl's *mafaen* at her own natal estate. As she gave that which asserted the woman's new claim on her marital estate, she also asserted her own prior *mafaen* claim on the girl's natal estate—the fact that the girl being married was still dependent on her. The importance of this lay in the fact that by marrying, the girl not only claimed her husband's land but also became the new *mafaen* to her own natal estate. Her father's sister would remain a *mafaen* but would be given less and have a less active role, though still demanding respect and still being able to throw the woman's brother off his land and indeed remove the woman from her position as *mafaen*. It was thus the *mafaen* on both sides who gave what was exchanged, asserting their claims to the woman's natal and marital estates.

It was also the *mafaen* who received what was given in return. The woman's side took what the man's sister or father's sister gave and

passed it on to the woman's father's sister, her *mafaen,* and thereby
asserted in return the woman's own *mafaen* claim on the estate she
was leaving. Likewise, what the woman's father's sister had given
was taken and passed to the man's side, making the woman's
counterclaim on his estate. It was to pay the *mafaen* off, to "shut her
mouth" (*ning e l'ugun*) as the woman moved in and took the land.

The exchange was thus reciprocal, one claim balancing the other
as what one person gave to assert one claim was used by another to
assert another claim (fig. 4). The garden food the woman's father's
sister gave to state her claim on the woman's natal estate was passed

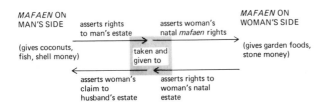

Fig. 4. The marriage exchange

on to the man's sister or father's sister to state the woman's claim on
her new estate, to satisfy its *mafaen.* In return, that *mafaen* gave
coconuts, fish, and shell money that were to state her claim on the
man's estate, but in so doing were given to the woman's father's
sister to assert the woman's claim as *mafaen,* a claim that was
countered by the garden food the woman's father's sister gave. The
mafaen claim on the wòman's estate was the woman's claim on
her marital estate; the *mafaen* claim in the woman's marital estate,
her claim on her natal estate. As the "our land belongs to someone
else; someone else's land belongs to us" dialectic works itself out in
the exchange, all claims and counterclaims are thus balanced out,
just as the woman's claim to the man's land was countered by his
claim to her children.

Everything in the *M'oy* ceremony was part of an exchange except
one piece of stone money and perhaps some baskets of food given by
the woman's father. This was her *gilab,* her personal "belongings"
and was to accompany her to her new home. It was thought to be
exchanged both for the care and food the woman would be given
there and, more important, for the land she would earn. It was an
advance payment on that land and was to act as an "anchor" (*yuluy*)

for her there. This piece of stone money could not be given away even after the woman died. Then it would become the "anchor" of the *mafaen* she had begun by marrying in. It held her and those she bore in their place on the land. Girls marrying into high chief estates would sometimes take a *gilab* of rights to land or sea area or even rights to specific services of lower-caste villages (roofing houses, collecting firewood). Because she brought an important *gilab*, according to one person, the *mafaen* line the woman began could endure longer than was normal, up to seven generations. Women marrying out of high chief estates into a slightly lower one could also take such a *gilab*, not as payment, but sort of as a "decoration" (*nunu*), an adornment to her.

What we have described was the basic form of the marriage *mitmit*. The initial *M'oy* ceremony was not particularly large, functioning merely to initiate relations between the two estate groups. Nor was it particularly competitive. Since excessive competition between the two estates would result in one side's losing, it was said that the ill feeling this engendered might weaken the marriage. It was also felt unwise to invest large amounts of labor and money when it was still unclear whether the match would endure. As the marriage lasted and the girl had a larger and larger investment in the estate, the exchanges became larger though retaining the same basic form.

The two *mitmit*s that followed the *M'oy* took place precisely at the point when the woman's investment became larger—as she became pregnant and after she had a male child—as her dependency upon her husband's estate as a place for her children likewise became greater.

About five to seven months after the first time the woman became pregnant, a ceremony was held, called *Falay* (medicine). The same exchanges of men's food from the man's side and women's food from the woman's side took place but in slightly increased amounts. The woman's side gave a piece of stone money called *maybil* (prayer) so that the man's side's ancestral spirits would be happy and make the child a girl who would be beautiful and marry into a chief's estate; they wanted their line, that of the clan and the *mafaen*, to continue and prosper. The man's side countered with shell money, also called *maybil*, so that the woman's ancestral spirits would be happy and give a boy who would be intelligent and strong in war; they wanted the estate to have heirs. The two sides likewise gave shell money to the magician (*tamerong*) who had come to facilitate the pregnancy by warding off evil influences and giving the woman medicine to drink. The shell money he received was to influence him in the same manner as the two sides tried to influence the ancestral spirits, so that he would use his power to make the child a girl or a boy. After the woman had her first child, there would no longer be an exchange of food, but simply a presentation of shell money to the magician so he would perform his medicine to facilitate the birth.

Sometime after the woman had produced children, and specifically after she had a male child, there would be a third and final ceremony called *Wel* or *Wayil*. This exchange was the largest and most competitive and could be executed only by those estates that were wealthy and also had extensive kinship ties. It was the final statement of both sides' claims on the child's father's estate. The heir to that land had been born, and it was up to the mother's people to solidify his place and up to the father's people to state the debt the child still owed to them. The mother's people had taken the land; its name had been given to their child, the child who, through his mother, was identified with them. They thus wanted to be sure that the mother and child were secure on the land, not in danger of being thrown off by the *mafaen*. In addition to all the garden food, they would also give a large, valuable piece of stone money called *rumag e ricib*, "to stick in a nail." It was to "nail" the child to the estate. It was not matched with anything in return, for it was to help pay for the land the child would receive. It would anchor the child to the land, as the *gilab* had anchored the mother, and would stay on the land long after the child had grown up, taken the land, and died. Against this claim on their land, the man's side would assert their prior rights to the land, their claim as *mafaen* and as the land's ultimate authority. People said that it was good if the woman's side won the competitive exchange so that the child would be secure on the land. But while some said that the woman's side could not win because fish and coconuts, what the man's side gave, were easier to get than garden foods, others argued the opposite.

The final *Wayil* ceremony placed the child in the vast constellation of claims and counterclaims that went with his ownership of the land his name bore. All those kinsmen who participated in the *Wayil* were connected to him by a relation involving land, and they all by their participation were aiming to show the strength of their claim to it. By having the child, the woman had completed a major part of the exchange that she had engaged in with the man, and the *Wayil* ceremony thus called into play all the relations that were implicit within the dialectic of man and woman, estate and clan. Up to the *Wayil,* the exchanges had involved mainly the *mafaen,* as they were concerned with the woman's moving from one estate to another. But after the birth of a male child, the total constellation of the estate's kinship relations became involved.

Having come to this point, let us consider precisely how this child-ego whom we have introduced was involved with the larger group by turning to an examination of the terms used to designate kinsmen.

4 "The People of the Estate"

A person's kinsmen formed the "people of the estate" (*girdien tabinaw*). All those in this group were designated by specific Yapese terms. Although many of the terms had fallen out of use as the mode of life on Yap itself had changed, and although information is imprecise at certain points, it is clear that those included in the "people of the estate" and terminologically labeled were included specifically because they played a role in the process by which a person came to hold land and pass it on. The "people of the estate," in effect, distinguished those involved in the dialectic of clan and estate as it operated about a particular person.

The terms we shall consider were those that an ego used to classify and refer to his or her kinsmen and were not usually used as forms of address. Some of them were also applied in other contexts to non-kinsmen. That, however, need not concern us here. While the terms mapped out all of those in an ego's system of kin, the kin system itself was defined not linguistically by a bounded terminology but by the social relations formed within the dialectic of clan and estate that we have been examining. The terms were used here primarily as labels for a system otherwise defined, as even the exceptions to this indicate.

For the purpose of this discussion, we shall consider the constellation of kinsmen about a male ego. We can begin by diagramming the set of kin that surrounded ego as he was involved in the basic relations of clan and estate that we have outlined—the exchange between man and woman, the transaction between clan groups, the balancing claims to land through the *mafaen* lines. In so doing we will use the usual genealogical notation, though indicating the special clan relation between mother and child by diagrammatically deriving the children from the clan women, as in figure 5.

Ego must first of all be placed at the center of the intersection of clan and estate. Ego was himself defined socially as the product of both lines. Through his father and his father's clan group, ego

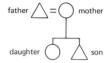

Fig. 5. "The people of the estate"

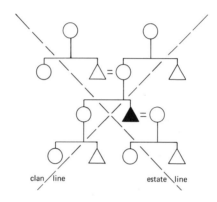

Fig. 6

received rights identifying him with the land they had held and representing the labor that had gone into developing and maintaining the estate. Through his mother and her clan group he received the *mafaen* rights identifying him with the land from which his clan line had just come and representing the labor his "people" had invested in developing and maintaining the clan. At the same time, ego's clan group was also the means of reestablishing and perpetuating the value of both lines, the clan line continuing through his sister and her children and the estate line through his wife and her children (fig. 6). Implicit in this intersection of clan and estate through ego was also, we saw, a set of lateral *mafaen* relations. To complete this basic configuration of ego's kin we must thus include ego's father's sister and her children, who were *mafaen* to ego, and ego's mother's brother's wife and her children, over whom ego was *mafaen*. Figure 7 effectively places ego at the center of a set of simultaneous claims through clan and estate, the one everywhere balancing the other. Opposed to ego and his mother's claim on his father's estate was the *mafaen* claim by his father's sister and her children; opposed to the claim of mother's brother's wife and children to their estate was his and his mother's *mafaen* claim; and

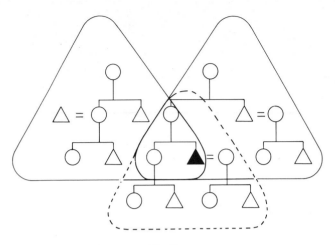

Fig. 7

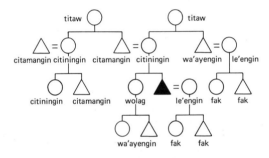

Fig. 8

opposed to the claim of his wife and her children to his estate, the claim of his sister and her children.

We can now fill in the terms ego used for these kinsmen. Looking at figure 8, we can see that the same terms (*citiningin/citamangin, wolag/wa'ayengin, le'engin/fak*) were used in the lateral *mafaen* system as in the lineal estate transmission system. Ego's "parents" (*citamangin/citiningin*) were not only his mother and father, but also his *mafaen*, his father's sister, her husband and children; ego's "wife" and "children" (*le'engin/fak*) were not only the woman he married and her children, but also the woman and children over whom he was *mafaen*, his mother's brother's wife and children (fig. 9). Further, in that the term for mother's brother and sister's child, *wa'ayengin*, [1] was explicitly said to refer to a kind of "sibling," ego's

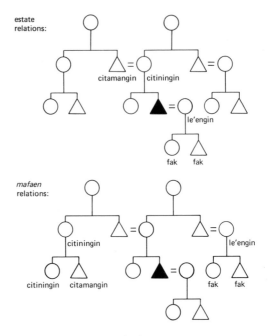

Fig. 9

"siblings" were not only those born of the same mother, but also those whose claim on the land ego continued through the clan as *mafaen*—his mother's brother—and those who similarly continued ego's claim to land—his sister's children (fig. 10).

The same terms were used because, from the perspective of Yapese social relations, the people in the two systems played analogous roles. They were both involved with transmission of the land rights that were fundamentally linked to a person's social identity. To transmit land was to transmit the labor that had been invested in it, the labor that formed the basis of all ascribed social status. This applied to rights passed through the clan as well as through the estate. Ego not only received his land from his parents and gave it to his wife and children, but also, and as part of the same process, he received land from his *mafaen* (his father's sister and her children) and gave it to those over whom he was himself *mafaen* (his mother's brother's wife and her children), who were thus also his "parents" (*citiningin/citamangin*) and "wife" (*le'engin*) and "children" (*fak*). Ego also shared his land not only with his siblings on the land, but

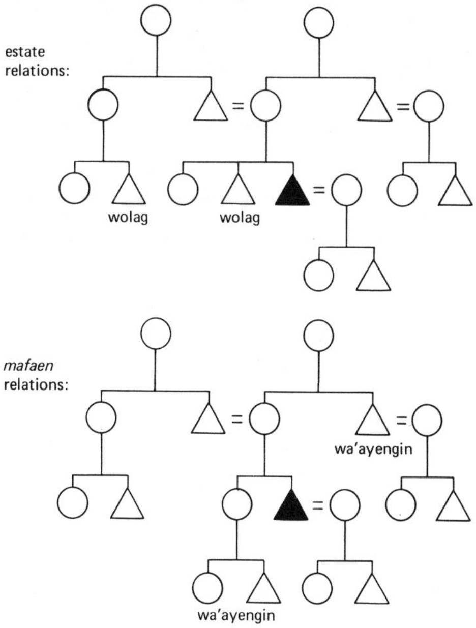

Fig. 10

also, through the *mafaen,* both with those who had remained on his mother's natal estate (his mother's brother) and those who would move off his natal estate (his sister and her children), who were consequently also his "siblings" (*wa'ayengin*). "Parents" generally were those from whom ego received his rights in land, "children" those who received their rights in land from ego, and "siblings" those who shared rights in land with ego.

The fact that each term referred at once to a relation ego had as a member of an estate and a relation he had as a member of a clan, however, also gave the terms themselves a dual meaning that reflected the dialectical nature of Yapese land relations. Each term itself contained the dialectic of clan and estate as it denoted at once two different kinds of relations, bringing them together as one. "Parents" were both those who gave ego the rights to the land he lived from and those who gave him the rights to the land over which he was *mafaen;* "siblings," both those who shared rights to the land ego lived from and those who shared rights to the land he claimed as *mafaen;* and "children," those who received the land ego lived from and those who received the land over which he was *mafaen*.

The only term that presents any complexity in this respect is the term for "father" (*citamangin*), which appears to be involved with the special sibling term for mother's brother and sister's child, *wa'ayengin*. We would expect that just as ego's mother and his father's sister were both "mother"—the one passing ego *mafaen* rights, the other, herself a *mafaen*, passing land—so ego's father and mother's brother would both be "father," each also giving land rights to ego. It was from ego's mother's brother, no less than from his mother, that had come the authority ego had as the guardian of the labor his "people" had invested in the land. Indeed, the role of mother's brother was said to be somewhat like that of a parent, being very similar to the role of ego's mother. Mother's brother, like mother, would act as a "navigator" to ego, giving advice and support and guiding him to the proper behavior that would insure his claim on his father's land. Yet ego's mother's brother was, in fact, classified by the special sibling term *wa'ayengin*. Although he was a "parent" in the same sense as ego's mother, he was also a "sibling" who shared a claim to land. The special sibling term appears precisely to mark the conjunction of these two roles involved in the mother's brother/sister's child relation. It made mother's brother a "sibling-father," thereby giving the notion of "father" a dialectical meaning and differentiating mother's brother from other "siblings."

The use of the term *wa'ayengin* was also important in maintaining the terminology's internal consistency. It avoided a terminological contradiction that would occur if ego called his mother's brother either just "parent" or "sibling." Since ego called his mother's brother's children "children" (*fak*) through his *mafaen* relations with them, it would be illogical for him to call their father, his mother's brother, "parent" (*citiningin*), as is shown in figure 11. Parents of those whom ego referred to as "children" were his "siblings," sharing rights with ego that they passed on together. If ego did call his mother's brother "parent," he would logically have to call his mother's brother's children "siblings," which would not fit the *mafaen* relations between them. It would also be somewhat inconsistent for ego to call his mother's brother "sibling" and his mother "parent" when his *mafaen* claim came from both of them. Just as father and father's sister were equated terminologically, so should mother and mother's brother be equated. The term *wa'a-yengin* neutralized both of these problems, making mother's brother at once a "sibling," and thereby terminologically consistent with ego's *mafaen* relation terms, and a "parent," equating him with ego's mother.

Still, the terminology here was not perfect. While ego's mother's brother was a "parent" like his mother, his mother was not a "sibling" like his mother's brother, the two being equated only as "parents" and not as "siblings." Even though ego shared a land claim with his mother as well as his mother's brother and those of the same clan were generally considered "siblings" (*wolag*), being ultimately derived from the same ancestral clan mother, people insisted that it would be extremely improper for ego actually to call his mother "sibling." This, they said, would be disrespectful, as it would lessen her importance and position in relation to ego. Having called her by a term for a "parent," one who contributed significantly to his social identity, he could not call her by a lesser term.

The people of the estate included more kinsmen than we have so far designated. Although the process by which one group earned an estate from another mainly concerned the people from whom they directly received land and those to whom they passed it, it was also seen to concern others who came before and after them in the clan and estate lines. These more distant kinsmen had less significance for ego, being increasingly peripheral to the specific exchanges he was involved in, and were consequently less well defined. As the discussion of the terms for kinsmen extended beyond ego's closer relations, people usually became less and less sure of the terminology and had to figure out what terms would be used. The shift away from a traditional form of life under colonial rule had also diminished the importance of maintaining the full sphere of kin relations, and some terms, it appears, had even been forgotten. It would probably be a

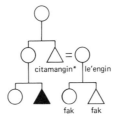

Fig. 11

mistake, however, to imagine that the terminology was ever conceived of as a strictly delineated and bounded logical system. It was

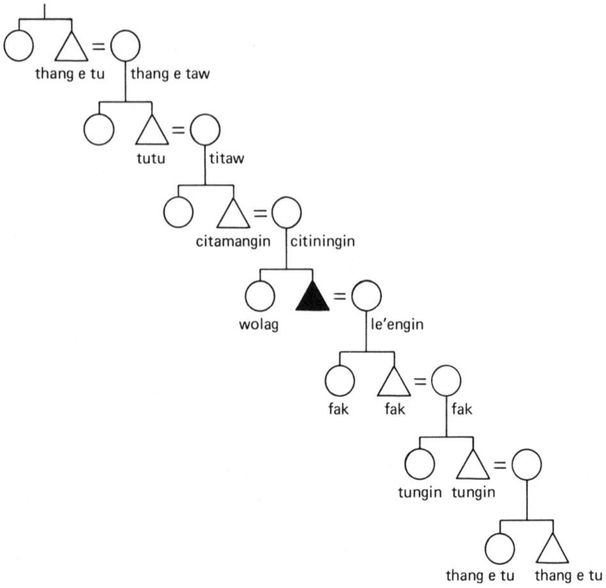

Fig. 12

fundamentally a pragmatic system whose basic structure was that of the actual social relations that surrounded ego and whose importance was that it could deal with the persons involved in those relations as the need arose.

Thus far, we have spoken of the transaction of the estate as occurring between three clan groups who came consecutively to live on the land. There were, however, more than three clan groups with interests in the estate. Having taken a wife and produced children, a man would watch his son marry, in turn, and bring yet another clan group onto the land. Were he to live long enough, into his late fifties or sixties, he might see the process repeated in another generation. As long as he lived on the land, those who came after him had to work for him and watch after him, fulfilling the "exchange of care" and doing for him what he had done as his own predecessors had grown old and died. The man's wife had a similar relation with her clan's successors. Beyond ego's parents, ego's father's parents (*tutu/titaw*) and his father's father's parents (*thang e tu/thang e taw*) were also terminologically differentiated, as were those who would be called by reciprocal terms for children's children (*tungin*) and children's children's children (*thang e tu*) (fig. 12).

The terms *thang e tu/thang e taw* were remembered only by a small number of people. Other terms for "great-grandparents," *tuwug, thang e tow/talmitow,* were offered by a few individuals, and in some areas no term at all was remembered, perhaps representing regional variation. Simply on the basis of age, however, it seems likely that some people would live long enough to become great-grandparents and that some term for them would exist. There was also some disagreement and uncertainty as to the proper reciprocal that should be applied to "great-grandchildren," whether it was *thang e tu/thang e taw,* simply *thang e tu,* or yet another term. I use *thang e tu* here because it seems to fit the pattern of not differentiating sex in "children" terms (cf. *fak, tungin*). The terms *thang e tu* and *thang e taw* were particularly appropriate, people pointed out, because the word *thang* means "to erase/extinguish." Being old and close to death, the role of ego's great-grandparents was almost over, the debts owed to them all but repaid.

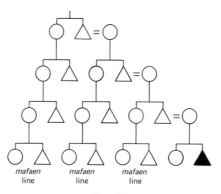

Fig. 13

As we have seen, the men who remained and grew old on the estate were only part of the clan group who originally worked to claim the land. Their sisters had all moved off the land and established the *mafaen* line that also represented their people's claim to the land. Connected with ego's father, father's father, and father's father's father were thus three *mafaen* lines with authority over ego, which can be diagrammed as in figure 13. The existence of the three *mafaen* lines effectively insured a regular succession of authority between clan groups. Even if the man who remained on the estate died young, the debt owed to his clan group would be overseen by the *mafaen*. It is easy to see from this also why a *mafaen* line was said to endure four generations, through a man's sister's daughter's daughter's children. The line ran parallel and counter to the different people who came to the estate, lasting for as many generations as the clan group might remain on the land.

The three *mafaen* lines that are mapped out above were distinguished by name. The names varied through the different areas of Yap, but it appears that the different names referred to the same *mafaen* lines. In the version used in Fanif municipality, the closest *mafaen*, father's sister and her children, were called the "new" *mafaen* (*mafaen ni be'ec*) because it had just arisen; the second *mafaen*, father's father's sister and her children, were called the "coconut shell" *mafaen* (*mafaen ni le'*) because like a hard coconut shell that would last a long time before disintegrating and disappearing, it had lasted and was still strong; the third and last *mafaen*, father's father's father's sister and her children, were called the "black bird" *mafaen* (*mafaen ni gapalou*) because it was more than likely that the woman who started it had died and her spirit had been "eaten by the black bird" (*ka languy gapalou ya'an*). The black bird referred to was a species of starling important in certain forms of divination.

These *mafaen* did not all have the same strength. The closest had the most authority and at a marriage was given the most and gave the most, because its claim to the land was strongest. Whereas the other *mafaen* had eaten off the land in the past at the various estate ceremonies, and the debt to them and their authority had been reduced, the "new" *mafaen* had just come to eat and thus would be given more and have a stronger voice in affairs. The furthest *mafaen*, the "black bird" *mafaen*, had eaten off the land for a long time, had received things at ceremonies in the past, and was almost paid off. It would have the least authority and would give and receive the least. The share given to it at a marriage *mitmit* also had another significance. It was called *maybil*, "prayer," and was offered so that the ancestral spirits would be happy with the proceedings. Since it was likely that the woman of four generations back would have died and become one of the ancestral ghosts of the estate, giving this to her descendants' ego thus propitiated her and the pool of ancestral spirits of which she was now a member.

The kinship terminology could quite easily designate those who were part of the three *mafaen* lines that had authority over ego. Since the *mafaen* represented the continuation of the claim of a woman's children on the estate, the terminology could express this simply by calling those who continued the claim the same thing it called those who first made it. In figure 14, those who were a continuation of ego's father and father's sister's people were, like them, *citiningin* and *citamangin;* those who were a continuation of ego's father's father and father's father's sister's people were, like them, *tutu* and *titaw;* those who were a continuation of ego's father's father's father and father's father's father's sister's people were, like them, *thang e tu* and *thang e taw.* It should be noted, however, that

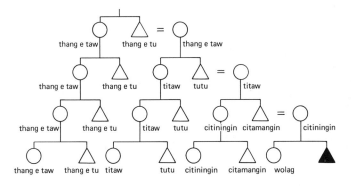

Fig. 14

as the outer *mafaen* lines were less significant to ego than his "new" *mafaen,* so the terminology itself seemed considerably less significant. While people would emphasize the "new" *mafaen*'s status as "parent" (*citiningin/citamangin*), they would inevitably have to work out the terms for the "coconut shell" and "black bird" *mafaen.*

The expansion of ego's constellation of kin to include further *mafaen* with authority over ego implied a reciprocal expansion to include those over whom ego himself had further authority as *mafaen.* As people were *mafaen* to ego, so ego, through his own clan relations, was *mafaen* to other people. One set of claims balanced the other, as is shown in figure 15. Just as there was a "new," "coconut shell," and "black bird" *mafaen* over ego, so he was the "new," "coconut shell," and "black bird" *mafaen* to others, specifically those on the estates of his mother's brother, his mother's mother's brother, and his mother's mother's mother's brother.

The terminology for these relations, however, was slightly less straightforward than that for ego's *mafaen*. Because the people in the clan line directly before ego each passed on to him a distinct claim in land, they were "parents" like the people in the estate line of which he was also a part (fig. 16).

The labeling of those in the *mafaen* line as parents was important in that it not only balanced the line of clan transmission against the line of estate transmission, but also gave the terms themselves their dual meaning with respect to the relations of the clan and estate. Thus *tutu* and *titaw, thang e tu* and *thang e taw,* were terms denoting both those from whom ego received the estate on which he lived and those from whom he received *mafaen* rights on the estate from which his branch of the clan had come. But it also posed a problem for the internal consistency of the terminology in the terms to be used for the various mother's brothers, the same problem we saw occurred if ego's mother's brother was called simply by a parent term. Although those directly before ego in the clan line were "parents" from whom he received *mafaen* rights, with respect to the *mafaen* relations themselves they were all his "siblings," who carried on a people's claim to land and shared authority over their common "children." This could again lead to contradictions in the terms used for these clan predecessors.

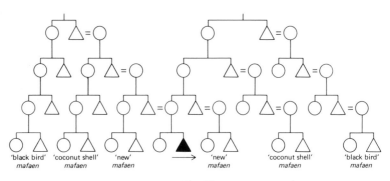

Fig. 15

If ego were to call his mother's mother's brother "grandparent" (*tutu*), then he would logically call his mother's mother's brother's children "parents" (*citiningin/citamangin*), and their children, in turn, "siblings" (*wolag*), as in figure 17. Yet ego was part of the *mafaen* line over his mother's mother's brother's estate and thus a "parent" to all those on it. He was part of the "new" *mafaen* to mother's mother's brother's children, and consequently their "par-

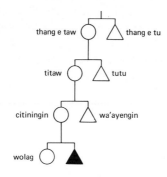

Fig. 16

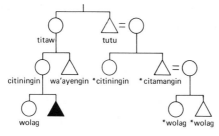

Fig. 17

ents" (*citamangin*), and part of the "coconut shell" *mafaen* to
mother's mother's brother's son's children and consequently their
"grandparent" (*tutu*). Reciprocally, they would be his "children"
(*fak*) and "grandchildren" (*tungin*), making mother's mother's
brother logically his "sibling" (*wolag*), as indeed he should be in
terms of *mafaen* relations (fig. 18). Mother's mother's brother was,
like mother's brother, both a parent and a sibling. But here, as in the
next generation with mother's mother's mother's brother, there was
no special term to resolve the two roles.

When I posed this problem, people would obligingly try to arrange
this part of the terminology in different ways, but they had little
success at achieving consistency. The terms for grandparents and
their siblings were felt to be the same, both on the side of land
transmission and on the side of clan transmission, but this could not
be made to fit with the terminology of *mafaen* relations. It was only
at the level of mother's brother, where the special term *wa'ayengin*
brought together the roles of parent and sibling, that consistency
was maintained.

It is highly unlikely that this terminological difficulty actually caused any problem to the Yapese. The difficulty was, first of all, neutralized with respect to close kin with the term *wa'ayengin* and was probably less perceptible with respect to more distant kin, where the existence of intermediary kin allowed a certain flexibility. It is further doubtful that the sort of rigid logical exercise we have performed here to expose the problem would have held much interest for them. Kinship was usually discussed with reference to specific persons; how, for example, one woman came from such and such an estate and married into another and bore a woman who was so and so's mother, and so forth. The terminology for the "people of the estate" that we have abstracted here was, above all, a reference system for specific persons as they participated in the processes of the clan and estate. And it was less important that it be logically perfect than that its structure fundamentally reflect those basic processes of Yapese life.

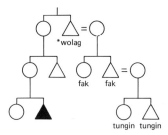

Fig. 18

It is not difficult to see how the mode of classification that applied to ego's predecessors on the estate and in the clan also applied to his descendants. As the *mafaen* line that continued ego's claim on the land endured until it became the "black bird" *mafaen* over ego's son's son's children, so those clan descendants who would make up that line were terminologically distinguished as such (fig. 19). In that it was from ego and his sister that his sister's children received their rights as *mafaen*, ego and his sister were their "parents"; but in that it was a right based on sharing and identity within the clan, they were his "siblings." The term *wa'ayengin* again appears to neutralize this difficulty by bringing together the roles of sibling and child in one term.

As ego passed his land to his wife and children, they would in turn become the beginning of a new *mafaen* line. Although these lines

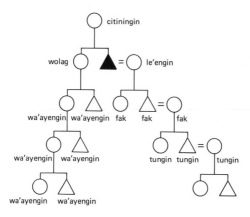

Fig. 19

were included in ego's constellation of kin, they were not distinguished as *mafaen* but simply as those to whom ego gave land, his "children" and their "children" (fig. 20). The lines through ego's female descendants on the land were not distinguished as *mafaen* because with repect to ego they were not such, being only those who had received land from him. There was no necessity, it appears, for him to differentiate them even by sex.

Finally, because ego passed on his estate through an exchange involving not only his own estate line but also his wife's clan line, his wife's close kinsmen became his kinsmen also. They were his *wecema'*, his "in-laws." *Wecema'* were those of another estate who, through the marriage of women either into or from ego's estate, had come to be connected to it. They included ego's sister's husband and the members of his estate, as well as his own wife's people. Ego could call his wife's mother and father *citiningin* and *citamangin*, "mother" and "father," but in so doing, people said, he was saying what his wife would say, for they were actually his *wecema'*. The same was true of ego's wife's brother's children. They would call ego "father" (*citamangin*) because he had authority over them through his wife, who was their *mafaen*. He could call them "child" (*fak*), but in so doing, he was speaking for his wife, saying what she would say and exercising her authority. There was also a special relation between ego and his wife's sister. If his wife died, ego could marry his wife's sister, a move that would be favored by her people in that it would maintain their hold on his estate. People gave this as the reason that wife's sister, while basically a *wecema'*, could also be called "wife," *le'engin*. [2]

With this we have mapped out the main lines of relationship through which the dialectic of estate and clan, land and people worked its way out in ego's life. Those who were included in ego's constellation of kin beyond this were included either as reduplications or purely logical extensions of the relations already established.

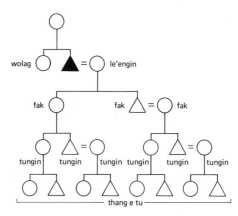

Fig. 20

The first group, those who reduplicated established relations, consisted of the siblings of the persons differentiated above. While it was possible to refer to a "younger sibling" (*tethingin*) and to differentiate between a sibling who was older (*ngani*) and had more authority and one who was younger (*wain*), siblings were generally equated in the roles they played. Since ego himself would not distinguish one sister from another in any fundamental way, the terminology used of all sisters and those descended from them was the same. Similarly, because ego and his brother shared a claim to the same estate and both passed it on to their children, not only were they considered "siblings" (*wolag*) themselves, but, as figure 21 shows, the wife and children of one were considered the "wife" and "children" of the other. If a man died and his wife remained on the estate, she would become the "wife" of the oldest surviving brother under the levirate, called *mun fungic,* a relation that could remain strictly formal or become as close as the man and woman wished. If the woman had already had children on the estate, she would be strongly encouraged to remain with them and accept the brother as at least a nominal "husband."

The sibling terminology diagrammed above was applied both to siblings of the same mother—said to be "of the same belly" (*yow ngayel*) or "of the same umbilical cord" (*yow ngabi*)—and to those born of the same estate by different mothers through the father's remarriage or, more rarely, through polygamy. Both sets of children would be "siblings," having the same relation to the father's estate. A man could take more than one wife, who would be called *tugeruw*, though only if he was wealthy enough to establish them separately on his land. The practice was said to have been rather unsatisfactory, frequently leading to fights between the two groups over possession of the father's land and status.

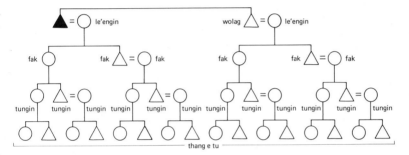

Fig. 21

The same principles of sibling identity also applied to other generations. Ego's father's brother and his wife were his "father" and "mother," passing land to ego; their children, who shared with ego a claim to the same estate, were his "siblings"; and so on, as in figure 22. In that ego's mother's sister and her clan descendants were, like ego and his mother, the *mafaen* to the estate ego's mother's brother passed on, mother's sister and her husband were "mother" and "father" and their clan descendants ego's "siblings" (*wolag*), those who shared the *mafaen* claim with him. The children of the men of the clan line through mother's sister were, like ego's children, not a part of that *mafaen* line and thus were distinguished appropriately (fig. 23). It appears that not only did mother's sister's line share a *mafaen* claim with ego, but they could also, under certain circumstances, actually become the *mafaen* over ego's estate as he passed it on. One person said that because he had no sister himself, his mother's sister's daughter and her children became the *mafaen* to his land instead. This makes excellent sense, because mother's sister's daughter was part of the same branch of the clan as ego and could well represent his and his mother's claim to their estate. Having outlined the way in which the terminology dealt with ego's mother and father's siblings, it should be unnecessary to go into detail concerning the brothers and sisters of more distant kin, since they would be handled in the same manner.

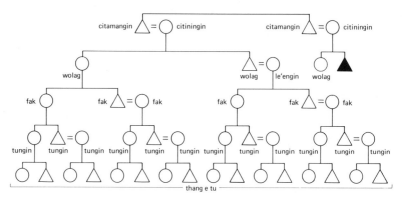

Fig. 22

The other group of persons who filled out ego's kin were those whose existence was logically implicit in the formation of the main lines of his relations that we have seen established but with whom ego himself retained no particular ties of land. The lines of kinsmen that extended back from ego through the estate and clan, for example, were not simply lines but were themselves at each step the product of the movement of clan peoples from estate to estate, and of estates from people to people. Implicit in the two lines was thus a set of claims and counterclaims to land following the path of that interaction. At every point, the lines were seen as the conjunction of balanced clan and estate relations (fig. 24). When I asked why it was that these people were considered ego's kinsmen when they had neither the importance nor the authority of ego's other kin, it was answered that he included them simply out of "respect" (*liyor*), both for them and for ego's more immediate kin related to them. They had, in effect, been part of the process by which the clan and the estate had come together to produce ego.

Yet part of this also appears to be a process by which the

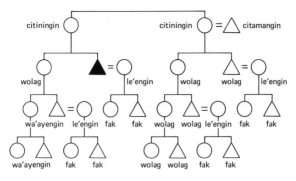

Fig. 23

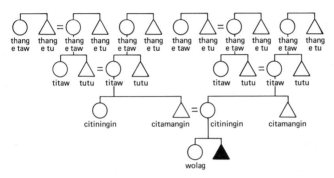

Fig. 24

categories of the terminology for those with whom ego did have actual social relations went on to create kinsmen by the force of their own logic, allowing, for example, the argument that because a man was classified as a "father," his child must be a "sibling," and so on. Those who could be included in ego's constellation of kin by force of terminology alone could thus gain the appearance of having the same status as those whose relations with ego had given the terminology its form in the first place. As ego's social relations created the logical categories of the terminology, so, in a sense, was it possible for the terminology to create social relations for ego.

It is difficult to tell to what extent this process occurred. People would consistently fill in those kinsmen diagrammed above, adding ego's father's mother's father and sister and his mother's mother's father and sister as *thang e tu* and *thang e taw* to complete the "great-grandparent" generation. But whereas some would relentlessly follow out the terminology step by step, making, for example, all children of those classified as "father" (*citamangin*) in the "new" *mafaen* line "siblings" and those after them "children" (*fak*) and those after them "grandchildren" (*tungin*) and those after them "great-grandchildren" (*thang e tu/thang e taw*), others would insist that such persons were not related, even though one could logically find a term for them. Still others produced the general rule that those descended from siblings were related as "people of the estate" through four generations, after which time they were not related and therefore could marry. While such a rule would include those with whom ego did have real social relations, it would also include those with whom he did not. This process could, of course, be a product of a situation in which much of the traditional kinship terminology had fallen out of use and become simply a linguistic artifact or, indeed, a product of the situation of obliging an anthropologist with answers to his questions. But more than likely, it simply gave people the option of extending the scope of their kinsmen in any situation where it was advantageous to do so.

This completes the constellation of kinsmen about a male ego (see fig. 25). The kinsmen about a female ego were fundamentally the same, with the addition of the term for "husband," *figiringin*, and of several special terms that marked the relations specifically between two women as they moved in and out of the estates. A woman who moved out of her natal estate and the woman who moved into her place would call each other *yanangin*, "sister-in-law." From the point of view of the woman who moved into the estate, *yanangin* was the woman who was *mafaen* to her children, and the term would thus continue down through the women of the *mafaen* line; the men of the line were *figiringin*, "husband," since the *mafaen* simply continued the role of the woman's husband (fig. 26). Finally, two women who married brothers would call each other *gurungin;* this, one person explained, was a kind of sibling, and indeed two such women did share their attachment to the same estate.

The "people of the estate," then, represented the dialectic of land and people as it was played out around each individual member of Yapese society. Although the discussion here has perhaps unavoidably been rather long and involved, we should not lose sight of the fact that in the end, the mapping out of ego's kin (fig. 25) amounts to nothing more than a further reformation of the diagram showing the interaction of clan and estate with which we began in chapter 2 (fig. 27).

The construct of the "people of the estate" was simply another

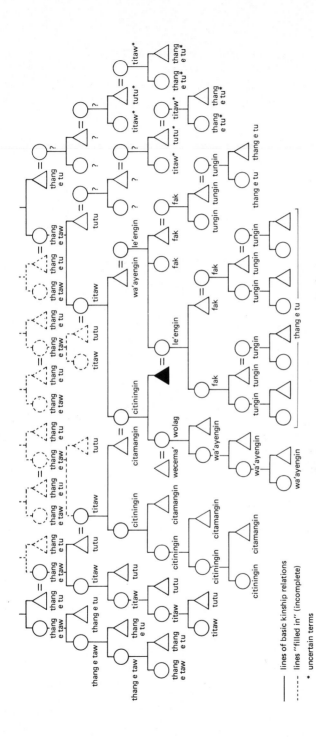

Fig. 25. The terms for kinsmen

—— lines of basic kinship relations

------ lines "filled in" (incomplete)

* uncertain terms

expression of that same ideology as it analyzed the relations by which the people on Yap had come to live and persist.

We have seen that people were born, received land, and themselves produced the children to whom they would in turn pass the land, all in the context of the relations of clan and estate. So, finally, did they die. When a person died, two groups of people would be affected—those who were closely related through the clan and those who had in one way or another received land from him or her. Those closely related in the clan would become afflicted with *wow*, the "smell of the dead" (*bun e yam'*). They were polluted by it and had to seclude themselves from other people, especially those of high status. Others in the dead person's clan would, if they heard of his or her death, abstain from eating fish for three days. To eat fish under such circumstances, people said, was like actually eating the deceased. Those who were afflicted with *wow* would mourn (*muwow/ya'al*) the dead, living apart and also abstaining from fish and obeying other restrictions. They would mourn the length of time it was thought to take for the body to decompose entirely, such that the "smell of the dead" was gone. Until that time, the deceased was in a transitional stage. Its spirit could not yet function well, being "heavy," weighted down by the still-intact body, moving confusedly above, unable to respond to whatever might be addressed to it.

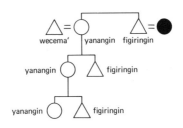

Fig. 26.

Those who received land from the deceased, either as a man's child or a woman's brother's child (over whom she had been *mafaen*), would join the clan in mourning. This was called "land mourning" (*muwow e binaw/ya'al e binaw*) and was explicitly to show respect to the dead person's clan. People explained that it was that people's land that was being inherited, and thus one joined them in mourning their dead. If one did not do this, the people of that clan who were the *mafaen* could expel the inheritor from the land for being disrespectful to those who gave it to them. It was not

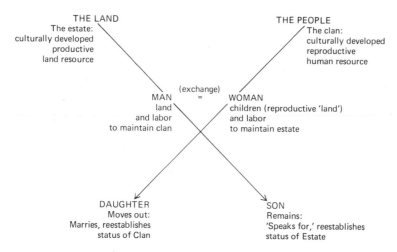

Fig. 27. The dialectic of clan and estate (cf. fig. 2)

simply a man or woman's child who would mourn, but their children as well. A person would mourn his mother's father because he gave her the land to which the person received the *mafaen* rights. Not all those who received land would actually mourn, but they would meet and decide who among them would join the dead person's clan in the mourning observances, not infrequently a young child. Only if a young person died without having married would there be no "land mourning," for he was not yet truly a landholder. It was also felt that the *wow* of such a person was not as strong as that of an older person, and thus only the closest clan relations, mother and siblings, would be affected.

When the *wow* had dissipated, the mourners had returned to normal life, and the deceased had become a responsive ancestral spirit of the estate, a portion of the dead person's land would be set aside. No one would be allowed to take anything from that land—which was usually the land surrounding his house, where there were mainly coconut trees, for a period of six months to a year. Of this land it was said, *ke aw e liw*. *Liw* means "place" or "position," as in the place a person occupies; it was said to "fall" (*aw*) on the land. During the time of the *liw*, the dead person was said to eat off the land that had been set aside. All the coconuts produced on that land were carefully collected and placed together. At the end of the *liw*, these coconuts were given to the dead person's *mafaen*, those descended from his father's sister; or, if it were a woman who had died, to her husband's *mafaen*. That *mafaen* was said to "eat the place of the dead person" (*kay e luwon fare yam'*), receiving what was his in death as he in life had received what was theirs. Significantly, only if an infant died before it had eaten food from the gardens (*gagan*), would no *liw* fall. Such a child was called an *achibay ni thay*, "a coconut bud that had fallen off the tree before it could develop." To have not eaten food from the land meant that the child was not yet dependent upon it and had not yet entered into the relations that attachment to the land entailed and that were expressed in the *liw* observance.

In death as in life, a person was placed between two claims on the land. He was mourned as one who had established himself on the land and who had passed on the land to others who were indebted to him and his people. But at the same time, he only came to take his place on the land, to merge with it as one of its ancestral ghosts, as he himself acknowledged his indebtedness to those who had held the land and merged with it before him. At every point, there were the relations of land and people expressed in the formula *tafedad, tafen be; tafen be, tafedad*: "our land belongs to someone else; someone else's land belongs to us."

5 "Pure" (*tabugul*) and "Impure" (*taay*)

The dialectic of clan and estate shaped Yapese social relations not only as it operated in the ego-centered world of the "people of the estate," but also as it affected all land and all people simultaneously. Except in a few special cases, Yapese culture allowed neither exclusive landholding groups nor immutable statuses. Rather, as we have seen, the movement of clans from estate to estate and estates from clan to clan set both land and people in a process of "development," treating them both as resources continuously transformable through labor. Since this process would at least in theory permit any clan people ultimately to hold even the higher estates or, less probably, any estate to be "developed" to hold the higher clan people, it asserted a certain kind of fundamental equality among clan groups and even estates. But more important, it also formed a basis on which they could be differentiated. Since different land and different people were all seen to participate in the same process, they could be compared or ranked in relation to one another through it, as they held different positions or represented different "levels of development" within it. The Yapese themselves defined such levels through a pair of terms that assigned comparative value to every piece of land and every person on Yap. They specifically differentiated land and people that were *tabugul*—sacred, high, pure, clean—from land and people that were *taay*—profane, low, impure, dirty. These terms were applied not only within the estate, but also within the village and between villages. They formed the basic vocabulary of a complex system of rank that pervaded all of Yapese life, strictly defining the social sphere in which a person could act, and everywhere establishing rigid patterns of authority and deference.

Although we have treated the estate so far as an undifferentiated whole, in fact it was importantly subdivided. Every man on the estate was *tabugul* with respect to his wife and children and took his food from *tabugul* land designated specifically for him; the woman and

her children were comparatively *taay* and likewise took their food
from *taay* land designated specifically for them. They each had their
own taro patches, gardens, food-bearing trees, and water supply,
and as soon as a catch of fish was brought to shore they would divide
it up into those fish that would be eaten by the man and those that
would be eaten by the woman and her children. The one could not
eat or drink what was designated for the other; they could not eat
out of the same pot; nor could the same pot or cooking fire be used
in preparing their food. A man viewed his wife's food with no little
disgust; to him it was *taay*—dirty and low. Were he to eat such food,
it was said that he would become ill, as would his wife, or anyone else
other than someone of similar rank, if she were to eat food from his
land. There were even restrictions as to who could work in which
garden or taro patch. If a large enough differential in rank existed,
those who were *taay* could contaminate *tabugul* land so that it would
cease to produce, while those who were *tabugul* could be themselves
similarly contaminated by *taay* land. The land of the estate did not
simply produce subsistence; particular parcels in it produced subsistence specifically for particular estate members. Since the people of
all the successive clan groups living at once on the estate each had
their own land from which to take their food and with it were *tabugul*
in relation to those who came after them, the estate was thus
effectively subdivided into a whole ranked series of different *tabugul*
and *taay* subunits.

It was the land in each of these subunits that was specifically
transacted between clan groups. Each clan group would earn the
land only bit by bit and parcel by parcel, advancing through a
succession of increasingly *tabugul* land units, receiving land that
belonged to those before them (to whom they were *taay*) and passing
on land they held to those after them (to whom they were *tabugul*)
(fig. 28). Once the people of a clan group reached the highest land on
the estate, they would have earned all of it, having at one time or
another held each of its ranked parcels. They would thus have
authority over the entire estate as well as the people who had come
after them and to whom they had provided land. The process of
estate transaction involved not only an extended series of different
clan groups, each with a prior and broader claim to the estate, as we
saw in the previous chapter, but a parallel extended series of land
units, each also successively representing a more inclusive claim to
the estate. People never actually held and used the estate in its
totality, but rather progressed through it slowly, earning rights to

different areas in it as they worked, gaining land that was increasingly *tabugul* and that gave them rights of authority and ownership over more and more of the estate, and becoming themselves increasingly *tabugul.*

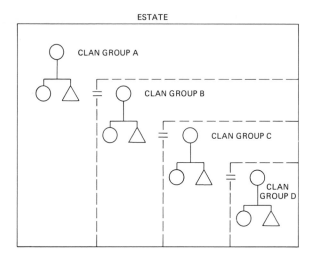

Fig. 28. Schematic diagram of the subdivision of estate land and people

What is first of all evident from these formulations around the concepts of *tabugul* and *taay* is that they expressed rank through exactly the same relation between land and people as that which expressed ascribed social positions generally. Just as people "spoke" for a "voice" inherent in land, so they came to hold a rank inherent in land. In both cases, the expression of a specific social position was contingent upon the possession of specific land. The fact that a person of certain social rank could be sustained only by land of equivalent rank, that the land would be productive only for certain people, was itself simply an assertion in another, perhaps extreme, form of what was stated generally on the estate by the basic dialectic of land and people: that on Yap, both socially and economically, the productivity of the people depended upon the productivity of the land, and the productivity of the land depended upon the productivity of the people. With rank expressed in the same way as status, the series of *tabugul-* and *taay-*ranked units of land and people within the estate essentially divided it into something like a hierarchy of individual "subestates," each having specific inherent powers and being held by members of different clan groups, one within the authority of another.

It was the relation of the people and land in these different "subestates" to which the terms *tabugul* and *taay* specifically referred. A man was considered *tabugul*—sacred, high, clean, pure—with respect to his wife and children because he and his "subestate" were seen to control the resources by which she and her children lived. The man would pass his wife and children the lower-ranking land he had himself already earned through his labor, land essentially subdivided off from the totality of land he had earned. They were thus dependent both upon the land's productivity with respect to him and upon his productivity with respect to the land. As the land had developed the man's resources and he had developed its resources, so the woman and her children would be developed in turn as part of that land was given to them. The man and his land were "sacred" in that they represented and con-trolled—and were responsible for—the estate's productivity with respect to his wife and children. He and his land were "high, clean, pure" in that it was from their greater resources and invested labor that the woman's "subestate" had been sectioned and set apart, a lesser and distinctly inferior fragment of it, made, as one person put it, out of that which was no longer of much consequence to the man himself. *Tabugul* and *taay* described the relationship of people and land to the means of production involved in the specific working out of the dialectic at the given level of social organization. For either people or land to be *tabugul* was for them to control Yap's productive resources in both quantity and quality, to have shaped the productivity upon which social life was based through the process of development, to be the source of that productivity and thus to represent, in this sense, the social order. To be *taay*—pro-fane, low, impure, dirty—was to lack that control, to be dependent, to have developed and been developed by the social order to a comparatively lesser extent. While the dialectic of estate and clan defined the process of interaction of land and people basic to Yapese social survival generally, the system of *tabugul* and *taay* defined the position of particular land and particular people in that process.

Every aspect of life within the estate was informed by the notions of *tabugul* and *taay*, from the gardens and taro patches and the planting and harvesting of food, as we have described, to the areas of personal living space and the performance of domestic activities. The traditional Yapese house was built upon a raised stone foundation and was divided lengthwise into *ban tabugul* (*ban* = "side"), which was considered *tabugul,* and *ban toor,* which was considered *taay* (fig. 29). Outside the house on the *ban tabugul* side would

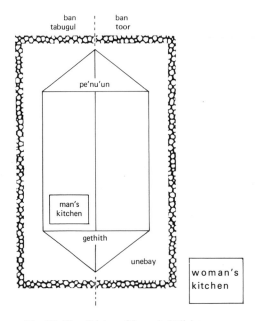

Fig. 29. The division of household living space

perhaps be the coconut and betel trees that would be used by the man of the estate. This area was specifically for him and was off limits to the public. Even his wife and children were to avoid the area, going there only when some task necessitated it. The house was also divided crosswise into the *pe'nu'un* and *gethith,* designations which refer specifically to the porches at either end of the house. The *pe'nu'un* was reserved for the man. If there were some serious matter he wished to discuss with other men, they might adjourn to that area. It was here, also, the most *tabugul* area of the house, that he would pray to the ancestral spirits. The *gethith* end of the house was the center of daily activity. The family spent much time sitting there talking and doing numerous small tasks, making rope, baskets, or grass skirts. The man would sit on the *ban tabugul* side of the porch, the woman and children on the *ban toor* side. The interior of the house was used only for storage, sleeping, and cooking the man's food. Inside on *ban tabugul* would be stored the family valuables, shell money, heirlooms, and implements of various kinds. Toward the *gethith* end would be the man's cooking fire and pots. In the middle of the *ban toor* side within the house there would be a hearth for warmth, and the man and his wife would sleep on either side of it, their heads toward *ban tabugul.* The woman's cooking fire would be outside on the *gethith* end, off the low stone platform (*unebay*) that surrounded the house.

Because she was *taay* in relation to her husband, a woman had to take special precautions in performing her duties in gathering or cooking her husband's food. Before cooking for her husband, a woman would wash her hands and put on a grass skirt that she had made specifically for that purpose, a skirt that she would not wear for anything else, lest it pick up contamination. Having put on the skirt, she would wash her hands again, holding them out so as to touch nothing but the things in the man's cooking area, and only then begin to cook. Before she went into the man's taro patch to get his food, she would put on another special grass skirt, usually one that she had used in cooking for her husband and that had become a bit worn out. It would not do for her to wear a skirt that she had taken into her own taro patch onto the land from which her husband would eat, for her land was *taay* in comparison with his. These were important obligations for a wife, and she would be watched by the man's mother and sister to see that she showed the appropriate respect to him in such matters.

The specific reason people gave for women being *taay* was that they menstruate and give birth. Menstrual blood was itself called *taay* and was the subject of the strongest disgust. During menstruation, a woman went to a menstrual area (*dapal*) outside the village proper. She could return only after she had ceased menstruation, had bathed, and had put on a new grass skirt. Even then, before she could reenter the house to cook for her husband she had to wait a few more days, bathe herself, and change her grass skirt several times. Similar constraints were put on a woman after childbirth.

That *taay* should be seen as a quality associated with a woman's reproductivity follows from what we have said above. *Taay* referred to both human and land resources that were essentially undeveloped, and it was specifically because a woman gave birth that she was seen as a reproductive resource. A woman who had reached puberty but who had not yet married and produced children was in this sense an *undeveloped* resource and therefore *taay.* It was only as her reproductivity developed on the estate, as she produced children who took on the responsibilities of the land, that she became less *taay,* less undeveloped, and more *tabugul,* a developed resource whose productivity both reflected and was reflected in that of the estate.

The Yapese distinguished five levels of womanhood. The names of these levels differed from area to area within Yap, though the distinctions made appear to be the same. The terms here came from Fanif municipality. Before a girl reached puberty, there were few restrictions on her, as she was thought to be not yet really defined as a woman. The young girl, or *buliel,* would generally eat with her mother, though she could take food from other people too. But as soon a she began to menstruate, strong restrictions applied to her. A *rugoth,* a young woman who had reached puberty but had not yet married and given birth to a child, was considered the most *taay* of women. At her first menses, she would be secluded away from the village in a special hut near the menstrual area—or at one of the lower-ranking villages, for the daughters of those who owned them. There she would stay for up to a year. This was a period of transition during which the girl became a woman. She was to do nothing except care for herself, bathe every day, eat and grow large and beautiful. She was so *taay* that she was even dangerous to herself. A special mat would be tied around her waist so that she would not put her hands on her grass skirt, considered extremely *taay* because of its proximity to menstrual contamination. Her hair was placed in a basket to protect it as it grew long and full, and she was given special sticks to poke through the basket to scratch her head so that contamination from her hands could not touch her hair and spoil it. To aid her development, the new grass skirt that she would put on after she bathed every other day was made of an especially fragrant grass (*Warub*). It was explained that just as one placed quantities of fragrant grasses around banana trees so they would quickly grow larger, so the strong-smelling grass skirt was to speed the girl's growth. Having become fertile but not yet productive, the girl was as yet in a state of nature, undomesticated, an undeveloped resource. One woman said that when the girl slept during her seclusion, she could not cover herself with a blanket or use any kind of sleeping mat except the crudest type made of palm fronds, sleeping "like an animal."

Even after she returned to the villag wearing the *marfaw,* the two black hibiscus threads worn about the neck and knotted so as to hang down between the breasts and to the small of the back as a sign of womanhood, she would, if unmarried, live for about a year in another special area of the village referred to as the *taminay* ("approach") or *tarugoth* ("place of the young girls"). She would use only paths that skirted the village and would avoid all sacred areas, high and chiefly estates, and meeting places for the chiefs. Were she to meet a group of men, she could pass them only after asking their pardon and then crawling past on her knees[1] so that they would not catch the *taay* smell of her body.

The food a *rugoth* woman would eat was considered extremely *taay*. If she remained unmarried on her natal estate, she would be given a plot of land from which to take her food and a separate cooking area and fire. Although she continued to eat off the land, since she was marriageable she now had to leave it. She could no longer even share her mother's food. She had no land that was really hers and was seen as a sort of "scavenger," eating just about anything. Things that grew close to the menstrual area would be given to her, or food of uncertain status that had come to the estate in an exchange. Were she to marry and move to her husband's estate, her status would remain the same until she produced her first child. Before that, she was not truly attached to any land—no longer a child but not yet a mother, the extreme state of *taay*.

After a *rugoth* young woman had given birth, she became significantly less *taay* and entered the rank of *dien* ("pregnant") women. Giving birth was an extremely important step for a woman and was compared with the advancement (*dowach*) of a man into the *tabugul* village eating classes that we shall examine later. The girl, one person explained, had then begun to produce on the basis of her husband's "planting." By producing children, she made her first important claim on the man's estate, providing that which demanded land in exchange. By entering the rank of *dien,* a woman would be freed from some of the restrictions on her movement, being able to use paths that went closer to the center of the village.

As a woman had more children and was actively raising a growing family, she again gained in status, entering the rank of *pithorang,* literally "beautiful," women. This was the time when she was physically the strongest and most productive. Once she reached menopause, she was designated a *puweluwol* and again gained in status, being no longer associated with menstrual blood and thus "almost like a man." Only then were all the restrictions on her movement in the village removed. The term further denoted a fully productive woman who had established herself on the land and thereby demanded respect. It could be used at a very general level in opposition to the term *rugoth* to indicate women who were socially established and had passed menopause as against fertile women who were still in the process of establishing themselves on their estates.

Finally, as a woman became older and her children reached the age when they could work the land to support her and her aging husband, as her son began to participate actively in the affairs of the estate, her position became even stronger. When she herself began to be cared for, she became a *pin ni pilibithir*, an "old woman," and had a very strong say in the internal affairs of the estate. As women progressed through these levels, they became more *tabugul*, considering those beneath them *taay*, taking their food from different parcels of land from those higher or lower in rank than themselves and keeping their cooking strictly separate, sharing food only with women of commensurate status.

People explained the process by which a woman became less *taay* in reference to her diminishing menstrual flow. A *rugoth* young woman, they said, would menstruate four to five days, but as a woman got older, this time would shorten until she ceased to menstruate altogether. Some people described it as if a woman contained only a specific amount of menstrual blood, and the more she lost, the less *taay* she became. The reason that was sometimes given for a woman's being raised in status after having borne a child was that the blood lost in childbirth left her less *taay*. Menstrual blood was directly related to a woman's fertility. A woman ceased to menstruate after becoming pregnant because, it was thought, the blood was being somehow used to help make the child. Menstrual blood was thus associated with a woman's position as a natural reproductive resource, being the essence of her natural reproductivity, and it was only as she used it in a useful manner or was finally rid of it that she ceased being *taay*.

Yet no matter how "developed" they became, women would never represent or "speak for" an estate or finally become as *tabugul* as the sons they bore. A mother would give her young son the same food she herself ate. As they were identified as part of the same clan group, they both had the same relation to the estate and, as she was *taay* with respect to the father, so was he. Like his mother, a son could never eat with the father. For him to do so, or for him to eat the same food as his father, people said, would mean that he had taken his father's position, something he could properly do only after his father died. A boy continued to eat with his mother until he put on the elaborate hibiscus-fiber belt (*kofor*) marking manhood and the assumption of manly responsibility. Then his mother would set up a separate cooking area for him. Although the mother would continue to cook for him and to take his food from her taro patch, she was said to separate him from herself to give him a bit more importance, even though they remained at the same level. Once the boy married, his wife would take over the responsibility of cooking for him and gathering his food. She was definitely *taay* with respect to him and would observe all the precautions of washing her hands and changing her grass skirt as she carried out her duties. Were his mother to cook for him again, she too would then make a point of washing her hands so his wife would see and follow her example. As the son came to hold more authority on the estate and was inducted into one of the *tabugul* village eating classes, he would eat from different and higher land than his mother, having himself become more *tabugul*. Even so, people insisted that this was not because the mother was prohibited from eating with her son. Their fundamental identification remained. The mother simply wished to reinforce the status and authority which her son had gained on the land and which she herself could not exercise.

Although the estate was sectioned into ranked units of land and people, it still retained its basic unity. At the same time that the estate was subdivided, it also incorporated a new "people." The different levels of *tabugul* and *taay* within it marked nothing more than different stages in the life cycle by which each successive clan "people" came to hold its highest land and status, the cycle by which the dialectic worked itself out in each generation. Within the estate, *tabugul* and *taay* denoted simply rank or order within a process, levels of development that were objectively continuous in the lives of those who passed through them. As the same principles that created the differential gradation of land and people within the estate were applied to more general levels of social organization, and as these estate ranks were placed in wider contexts of village and district, however, *tabugul* and *taay* came to denote entire ranked social strata that were increasingly discontinuous as they were broad, increasingly absolute, and separated from each other.

While those who held specific estates represented and "spoke" for the labor invested in them, certain estates were seen to have authority over others and to encompass them, to "speak" for them at the level at which they were part of an aggregate of estates in a village or village section. Just as the people of the estate were thought to become more *tabugul* and to hold more *tabugul* land as they came more and more to represent the estate and what it had become, so the different estates themselves were considered more *tabugul* as they held authority over others in the village, representing it as a whole.

Certain estates within the village had the status of *pilung,* "chief." People explained the term by saying that it meant "to give (*pi*) voice (*lung*)." The *pilung* spoke for the group, those who lived in a certain area, village, or village section. The people in it could act together as a group for the general welfare only as he brought them together and spoke for them. His voice both represented all their voices and commanded them; it was to reflect the consensus and to command the group. The term *pilung* was also explained by reference to the word *ulung,* "group." It was only the *pilung* who could bring people together so that they could act or work as one.

The *pilung*'s authority came from his "ownership" of a certain area as its *suon.* It was frequently said that the land had all belonged to the *pilung* at one time, and as the population had grown and the land had been subdivided, those belonging to the estate that had originally held the land came to have authority over others. As the land was subdivided, and more and more village sections and sub-sections created, one estate came to have authority, to be *suon*, over another. The right of *suon*ship could also be gained as a result of warfare. The word *suon* was explained to mean "the position of sitting." Sitting was the position of authority in which a person directed activity while others got up to move about and work. Such was the *pilung,* the one who allowed the people who lived within his authority to work together. The word *suon* also denoted the act of sitting upright; this, one person explained, referred to the fact that until the *pilung* spoke, it was as if the voice of the group "slept"; nothing could happen until the *pilung* took the initiative.

The *pilung* was seen to be in a position analogous to that of the father on an estate and could be referred to as a "father" (*cita-mangin*). It was his land that people lived on and to him that they owed their labor. When a woman and her children worked to earn an estate, they were said to work so that they could *suey* that land, "sit" as authority over it. Just as one group followed another on the estate, each becoming *suon* over the next, so the *pilung* was *suon* over the land of which the estate was a part, and so there was another higher *pilung* who was *suon* over him. The authority of a *pilung* of a section of a village would be encompassed by the authority of the *pilung* of the entire village, which would be encompassed by the authority of the *pilung* of a group of villages, and so on. It was considered extremely bad to say, "I am *pilung*," because there was always someone who was higher, *suon* over that *pilung*, and thus his *pilung*. While a man could finally come to speak for the land at one level, someone else spoke for it at another; the relations of people and land within the estate thus also continued hierarchically outside of it.

There were also estates in the village that had some *pilung* status because of a specific duty they would perform, either in helping carry out the responsibilities of one of the higher chiefs or in performing religious or ritual duties. Still others had authority in activities such as gardening or types of fishing or warfare, and still others were magicians (*tamerong*) with competence in specific matters—war, fishing, dancing, and so on. By controlling such specialized authority or technical information, they too controlled productivity and were thus also *pilung*.

It was impossible to get a full account of village social organization because a great many estates had been abandoned and their statuses forgotten. But it appears that what gave these different village statuses their overall coherence and unity was less a fixed pattern of authority than the general notions of *tabugul* and *taay*. As they variously represented the productivity of the village, the people and land within it could be differentiated on the same basis as within each individual estate. The more a man represented the productivity, the history of development, of the entire village—being himself, in a sense, responsible for such productivity through the labor invested during the development of his clan line to *pilung* status— the more he was *tabugul*; the less he represented that productivity, the more he was *taay*. A similar line of reasoning applied to land. At the level of village organization, there was thus again a system of eating categories that equated those of the same status and power and strictly separated others.

The men who came to speak for the more powerful estates in the village not only were *tabugul* within their own estates but were *tabugul* at a general village or public level as well, as was the land from which they took their food. In comparison, the men with no real village authority and the land they ate from were all considered *taay*, no matter what positions they might have in their own estates. Since only those men who had equivalent authority within the village and who ate from land of equivalent status could share their food or eat together, they essentially formed a separate eating class, as did others with similarly equivalent authority, or lack of it. The result of this was a system of village eating grades, the *yogum* (or variously *yegum, togum,* or *mokun*), that distinguished the rank of all men of all estates. The ranks determined the way food was eaten, as well as the public division of food at a religious ceremony or after a communal fishing expedition. The Yapese generally would hesitate to eat outside their own estates where they could not be sure that they were eating food appropriate to their rank that had been properly prepared or where it might seem that they did not have enough food at home. Close friends or relatives might, however, eat together. The sharing of food basic to the *yogum* took place most frequently in the process of distribution and not in actual consumption.

The names of the *yogum* grades differed from area to area, and it was impossible to get full accounts of them everywhere. Nevertheless there is good evidence that in most areas seven *yogum* levels were established. The names used here[2] were from Ateliu village:

tabugul	*munthing*
	lan e mallal
	beec
	toru
	yangac
	tan e yangac
taay	*magath e lili*

Only land and people classed in the top three *yogum* (*munthing, lan e mallal, beec*) were *tabugul* at the villagewide level. Placement in the ranks, as indicated, took two factors into consideration: the man's position within the internal ranking of his own estate and the position of his estate wth respect to others in the village. Since a father was *tabugul* with respect to his son, the two men could not occupy the same *yogum* grade. The son had to remain at least one grade behind his father. Only the men of the highest estates could progress through all these levels to the top, *munthing.* Men of other estates, with lesser "voices," would be able to proceed only to a level equivalent to one of the sons of the top estate, for example, *lan e mallal* or *beec.* The oldest man of that lesser estate would reach that level and stop, his sons taking the ranks below him. The limiting factor on the final point of advancement in the *yogum* was the possession of a ranking taro patch (*muut*). For a man to enter the *munthing* level, for example, his estate had to possess a taro patch that was specifically designated as being of the *munthing* level. It appears that not all villages had all ranks. A lesser village, one under the authority of the chief of another village, might have no estates that could enter the top class or classes.

While the *yogum* levels marked gross increments in status, the scale was, in fact, continuous, and there were discriminations within the levels themselves with respect to age and rank. Two men of the same rank could eat together, but if they were widely separated in age, they could only eat food cooked in the older man's pot. The older would not eat food cooked for the younger. When certain foods were distributed, there was also a specific way in which the portions would be given to show rank; the more *tabugul* portion of a fish, for example, went to those higher in status within the same *yogum* level.

Like advancement in status within the estate, advancement in the *yogum* classes was earned. The chiefs would watch the younger men as they worked and carried out their responsibilities, and when they felt it appropriate they would tell a young man he could advance. The significant step for a man was to move into the top three *yogum* levels and become *tabugul* with respect to the village as a whole. A man could move into these *tabugul* ranks only if his estate owned a taro patch for that rank and if his father had vacated the rank either by death or by his own advancement. No one I talked to knew how taro patches had come to be of any of the top three levels, nor were there any physical characteristics or markings that would differentiate them from other taro patches. Whereas it was possible to build taro patches to be used by the lower four levels, the taro patches of the top three were sacred ground that either was part of the resources of the estate or was not. It appears that with few exceptions, all estates in a village were able to attain at least the lowest rank of the top *tabugul* ranks (*beec*). The two top eating classes would be reserved for the most important estates of the village, those with important leadership or religious duties.

The person who moved into a *tabugul* rank had to buy his way in, presenting shell and stone valuables to the chiefs and those in the *yogum* level he was entering in a ceremony called *dowach*, where he was first given a share of their food. This represented a rather large investment and was a demonstration of the social power of the person who was to enter the higher class. It was said that some people could not afford to advance into the highest class they were entitled to, and therefore had to stay in a lower one.

To enter the top three *yogum* was to make the transition to a state of being inherently *tabugul*. After a man had gone through the *dowach*, he could no longer come in contact with the dead, nor would he be contaminated by *wow*, the "smell of death" that afflicted those related to a person who had died. By becoming *tabugul*, the man moved from the realm of the physical and profane to that of the spiritual and sacred. Those of the highest rank, *munthing*, were considered to "eat with the spirits" (*yow be abic e kan*) and their taro patches were thought to produce "spirits' food" (*gagan e kan*). Those of the top three *yogum* ranks were generally the "men," *pumoon*, of the village and were respected as *tabugul*, whereas those in the lower ranks were the "boys," *pagal*, and were still *taay*. One person said that before a man entered the ranks of the *pumoon* and became *tabugul*, he could not really speak as a high chief because "his mouth was *taay*." After he had gone through the *dowach* he could exercise authority because "his voice had become *tabugul*." There seemed also to some extent to be the sense that those who had become *tabugul* were wiser and more knowledgable in cultural affairs—even more worldly, having been groomed in the lower ranks to graduate finally into the ranks of those who conducted social affairs on Yap.

Like the living area space within the estate, the village was divided into areas that were *tabugul* and *taay*. The estates of high status and the taro patches of the top *yogum* were said to usually be near the center of the village. These areas were generally prohibited to young, fertile women and people of the lower village ranks. The top *tabugul* taro patches were definitely off limits to such people, and only men or women who had ceased to menstruate could work them and collect food from them. Lower estates and taro patches were more and more toward the outskirts of the village, near the paths for the *rugoth* women and lower villagers. The taro patches would furthermore be arranged so that the water flowing through them went into the higher ones first so that it would not pick up contamination.

For a young, fertile woman to go into or near a *tabugul* taro patch would cause the land to become "polluted" (*tungaf*). The taro would cease to grow well, and the woman herself would become sick. The land would "spit at her" (*rathuw e but ngak*), and she would never become pregnant. Worse, if a fertile woman ate food from one of these taro patches, it was said, she would become very sick and would cease to menstruate. Were she a young woman who was still extremely *taay*, she might even die. The same was true of men of the top *yogum* who ate food from lower taro patches. The seriousness of the illness that would strike them depended again on the disjuncture of status between the food and the person. It was said that men would get sores on their throats and become unable to eat, that blood would run out of their mouths, and that they could even die. While *tabugul* food could make a *taay* woman cease to menstruate and lose her fertility, *taay* food would give a man a kind of fatal "fertility," making blood flow from his mouth.

Few estates had great enough land resources that each level we have described could have its own separate land, and it was possible for people in some different classes to share access to the same taro patch. This was done on the rationale that a person of one level could "throw away" (*n'ag*) food to a person of the next level down. It was explained that they would "throw it away" much as one would throw away something no longer needed or wanted and have it retrieved by others. Thus a *pin ni pilbithir* woman might take her food from the same taro patch as her son's wife in the *puweluwol* class beneath her, the younger woman perhaps caring and cooking for the older. But they would say that the food was "thrown away" from one level to the next and would still maintain separate cooking fires and pots, a woman always remaining *tabugul* with respect to her son's wife and unable to eat with her. It was not proper, however, for women who were still fertile to share a taro patch with women who had reached the menopause, though each group could share among themselves. Similarly, men who had entered the top three *tabugul* ranks could not share with those who had not entered. *Munthing*-level men, being the highest of *tabugul* men, would usually have their own taro patch, however small.

The *yogum* system, then, placed the hierarchy of individual "subestates" of the internal estate ranking system into a wider village context. In so doing it separated the village order, in turn, into a hierarchy of distinct "suborders," entire broad strata of land and people considered to be qualitatively different from each other. The repeated subdivision of resources was seen to have set up one order inside another, creating different strata that lived from land sectioned off from that of an established landholding stratum— "thrown away," as one person put it, alluding to the practice mentioned above—that produced, consumed, and exchanged their food separately, that were to be kept apart both physically and socially. As the notions of *tabugul* and *taay* had, at the same time, been applied on a village level to indicate the relations between estates, they had themselves become more categorical and absolute. Since some estates had more authority and higher-ranking *yogum* land than others, some, indeed most, estates were excluded from the higher *tabugul* ranks. Those ranks were thus set apart no longer as stages in a universal life cycle, but as exclusive orders accessible only to a few. *Tabugul* and *taay* at this level became less continuous and more strictly opposed, more separated in that they were more separate. Even so, the separation was not complete, since all estates had land providing rights to at least the lowest level of the *tabugul* ranks. It was only as *tabugul* and *taay* were applied to intervillage relations in a system of village ranks that the discontinuity became extreme, subdividing Yapese society as a whole into two totally separate and opposed "subsocieties," one inherently *tabugul* and the other inherently *taay*.

Most broadly, villages on Yap were differentiated as *pilung* or *pimilingay*, a distinction that was once again based on landownership. The *pimilingay* villages were situated on land that belonged to a *pilung* village, not simply in the sense that the *pilung* were *suon* over it, which they were, but also in the sense that the village land was seen as being actually part of the land held by the estates of the *pilung* village. The *pimilingay* had no land of their own and were said to have had to ask for land from others. Two general explanations were given as to how it came about that they were landless. Traditional Yap was overpopulated. The result of this population pressure was that some people ran out of land before others and were forced to seek land from those who still had it, settling on an area of less desirable land that had not been developed. Other people, it was said, had become landless because they had committed some offense and been forced to flee. They would take refuge in another part of Yap and convince the people there to protect them and provide them with land and food. Whereas the term *pilung* referred, as we have seen, to those who owned land and had a "voice" in social affairs, the term *pimilingay* was explained as "those (*pi*) who run (*mil*) to it (*ngay*)," the "it" being the estate of the *pilung* who provided them with food and land.

By receiving land, *pimilingay* came to be in the same position as a man's children and were considered as such, as *fak*. They were said to be the most important of children, being like the oldest of all a person's children, responsibility to them coming first. Like children, the *pimilingay* owed their labor to the parent estate that owned their land. There were two labors that stood out in the service of the *pimilingay* to their *pilung:* providing roofing for his house and burying his dead. People said that providing a roof was the first responsibility of a child, the basic act of the exchange of care which marked a father-child relationship, providing protection for the father as the father had protected the child. While putting a roof over the father was the first responsibility, burying him was the last. The body of the dead person, as well as the place where it was buried, was considered extremely *taay*, and it was for the *pimilingay* to deal with the body, to carry it out of the village to the burial spot.

Beyond these two basic responsibilities, the *pimilingay* were to help their *pilung* in whatever task they asked, be it building a garden or a taro patch or making lime for betel-nut chewing. The *pimilingay* were also to produce the basic manufactured household and personal articles used by their *pilung*, cooking pots, sleeping mats, combs, and dyed fiber, and could be called upon to do simple services such as collecting coconuts or firewood or poling a canoe. All these labors were called *lung tabinaw* or *lung binaw*, "the voice of the estate" or the "voice of the village." The labor was exchanged for the use of the land that was spoken for, owned, by someone else. The *pimilingay* estates did have a "voice," but it was limited to dealing with the affairs of its own village. In matters of larger scope, the *pilung* would speak for his *pimilingay*.

Pimilingay were generally described as living off in the bush on land that was poor and not very productive, having few resources. They were said to have only a few taro patches and to depend more on garden (*milay'*) food. Their villages were for the most part inland, away from the more fertile coastal land. They generally had no sea rights of their own. They could use the sea areas owned by their *pilung*, but even then they could not do the more complex forms of net fishing. They were limited to hook and line (*lum'aeg*), a stick for feeling for fish under rocks (*thilom*), small hand nets (*c'eu*), and a bigger plowlike net fish scoop (*k'ef*); the lowest *pimilingay* villages would also use poison (*yub*) and a noose to catch moray eels (*gabass*). Those forms of fishing that involved more complex technology, the manufacture of nets, and the coordination of more people were considered higher and the prerogative of the higher *pilung* only. The *pimilingay* fished only in a crude way. They were more like women, living off the land. Were the *pimilingay* to run out of food, they would then go to their *pilung*, who was obliged to provide it for them from his own gardens.

Both physically and socially, the *pimilingay* existed on the periphery of Yapese society, surviving from marginally productive land and technology granted them by the *pilung*. The *pimilingay* and

their villages were considered the extreme of *taay,* a totally dependent subsociety beneath the established order. It was at their villages
that the dead would be buried, some even within the village proper, a
fact which not only marked the village as *taay,* indicating its position
with repect to the *pilung,* but also made it *taay.* No person of a
pilung village would eat food cooked by the *pimilingay* in their pots,
and only women and young boys would eat food grown on their land.
When a *pilung* girl first began to menstruate, she could be sent to a
pimilingay village for her period of seclusion. She would take her
food from their land, though she would not eat from their cooking
pots but brought her own with her. No man of a *tabugul* eating class
would, of course, having anything to do with food from such a
village.

There were also some kinds of food that were inherently *taay* and
therefore considered *"pimilingay's* food" (*gagan e pimilingay*) or
"woman's food" (*gagan e pin*). Men of the *tabugul* eating classes, or
even older women, would never eat them. The common attribute of
these foods (e.g., sweet potatoes: *komut;* yams: *thaep, ar, dol*) was
that they grow relatively wild, requiring little or no care. Some you
would plant, it was explained, and they would grow all over the place
by themselves. Others you didn't even have to plant (e.g., *rok*). Such
food also included two kinds of taro (*cath* and *yumeyume*), which
were so hardy that they required no care. It was said that one need
only plant a few in a taro patch, and a year later it would be full of
them. If a heat spell threatened all other kinds of taro, these would
still be healthy. You could even pull them out by the roots and throw
them somewhere and they would still grow. The connection is
obvious: *pimilingay* and younger women were *taay* in the same sense
that these foods were *taay.* Their survival did not depend on any
investment of labor; they were wild, undeveloped, and undomesticated, existing outside of society in a state of nature.

While *pimilingay* were considered "children" of the *pilung,* the
general attitude of the *pilung* toward them was one of undisguised
contempt and scorn. Some people could roll off the word *pimilingay*
as if they were referring to the lowest and most contemptible of
creatures. During traditional times, one could immediately tell a
man of *pimilingay* status by his dress. *Pimilingay* were forbidden to √
wear a comb in their hair, as did the *pilung,* to carry any but the
roughest basket, or to use several other articles of personal decoration. They would also have to move out of the way of *pilung* villagers
on a path and could walk past a group only by stooping as they went.
Pimilingay could come into the *pilung* village if they had some

business with their *pilung* or were to perform some work for them, but in so doing, they had to follow the paths used by young, unmarried, and menstruating women and those carrying the dead, paths that avoided the higher taro patches, sacred areas, and chiefs' houses. Even when they arrived at their *pilung*'s estate, they could not sit on his porch but had to sit a distance away from the house, like a *rugoth* young woman. Were they given food, they would eat it away where the *rugoth* ate. *Pimilingay* lived in the lowest and most *taay* villages on Yap and were treated accordingly. In speaking of them and their habits, people of the *pilung* status would say that they were just like animals and hardly people at all.

Intermarriage between *pilung* and *pimilingay* was generally prohibited. There was nothing that could benefit a *pilung* woman in a *pimilingay* village, it was said, and she would simply be wasting generations of her clan's labor by marrying down into it. Nor, equally, could a *pimilingay* woman bring anything of value to a *pilung* village. Those born of *pimilingay* rank were fixed there, isolated from the *pilung* as categorically *taay*. The discontinuity between *tabugul* and *taay* had, at this level, become absolute.

Although the dichotomy between *pilung* and *pimilingay* was absolute, drawn between those who owned their own land and those who lived on others' land, there were gradations of village rank within those classifications. Like ranks within the estate and the village, the categories of *tabugul* and *taay* villages admitted of several levels. At this point, however, my information about the traditional system becomes inconclusive, even with respect to the ranks themselves. The village rank system had to do with the authority of the chiefs, and as that collapsed with depopulation and colonialization, so it seems did the relations of the rank system. People had little experience with those relations and could give only fragmentary accounts. While the village rankings were discussed differently by different people, the general pattern that emerged was a familiar one, having the same form as the *yogum* ranks:

pilung/tabugul	*bulce/ulun*
	methiban/tethiban
	dourcig
	milingay ni arow
	milingay
	yagug
pimilingay/taay	*milingay ni kan* (*yagug ni kan*)

There was considerable disagreement among people on several points. The main problem came with *methiban/tethiban.* Some thought that they were two levels, *methiban* being higher than *tethiban,* while others argued for the manner shown here, saying that just as *bulce* and *ulun* were basically the same level, but terms that differentiated villages of one political alliance from the other, as we shall see later, so *methiban* and *tethiban* were of the same rank but different alliances. There was no way to resolve this question factually, and I have chosen the solution that the analysis of other data indicates should be correct.

There was a similar disagreement on whether the *pimilingay* ranks of *yagug* and *milingay ni kan* were two separate levels or simply different terms for the same level. Here I was able to satisfy myself fairly well that they were indeed separate levels by differentiating the relative status of specific villages in terms of their different practices and obligations and then trying to get at the names of the different levels. In just giving the names, people tended to lump them all together as equally low. One might perhaps think that the easiest way to solve the problem would be simply to ask the ranks of different villages. That, however, solved nothing. Rank was a sensitive social issue, and there probably had long been a tendency to blur the distinctions so that one's own village appeared as high as possible. In any case, most people were themselves confused on the matter.

The pattern of power and status that the ranks reflected, however, was fairly clear, following that of the estate and village where the higher ranks were more *tabugul* and had authority over the lower. The *bulce* and *ulun* villages were the high chiefs within a given area and were *suon* over it. It was they who ran the political affairs within that area, all other villages being considered under them, their "children" (*bitir*). Directly beneath them were the *methiban* and *tethiban* villages. Although they appear to have had all the rights of the *ulun* and *bulce*, for example, rights to certain prestigious forms of fishing, and would participate with them in the important religious observances of the area, they did not have the same political power. Under them were the *dourcig,* the lowest of the *pilung* villages. They were clearly under the authority of the higher villages but still one rank away from the *pimilingay.*

The pattern of eating relations between these three ranks of *pilung* villages appears to have been the same as that between the three *tabugul* ranks in the *yogum.* Just as a man of a higher eating class could not eat with a man of a lower one but could "throw away" food to him, a man of a higher village could not eat food from the pot of a man of a lower village, even though they had reached the same *yogum* rank. The lower man could come and eat with the man at the higher village. The reason given for this was that, in general, the taro patches of the lower village were *taay* with respect to those of the higher. But this was not extended to those of *pimilingay* villages, who could in no way eat with the men of the *tabugul* eating classes and appear to have had their own separate *yogum* ranks and ceremonies.

The highest *pimilingay* rank, *milingay ni arow,* was in a medial position between *tabugul* and *taay. Arow* was a designation used for the *pilung* villages, indicating the area of fertile land just back from the sea, where *pilung* villages were situated.[3] This rank was both *pimilingay,* in that it referred to villages on land owned by some *pilung* village, and *arow,* in that such villages also had some of the status of the *pilung;* the term itself means *"milingay that is arow."* They were not required to bury the *pilung*'s dead or roof the houses of anyone except those who were *suon* over major areas of their village. Some *milingay ni arow* also had rights to higher forms of fishing, being able to use large nets, although they still had to give some of the catch to their *pilung,* as they were said to be fishing for him. The *milingay ni arow* did not provide manufactured articles like the lower *pimilingay.* When they went to their *pilung,* they would bring food or betel nut or a certain sea clam (*unguwol*) that they might exchange for fish. They were also allowed to wear combs in their hair, the mark of *pilung* villages. Several people explained that these combs were for scratching their heads when they carried the food of their *pilung* during a journey, another of their duties. Since they were *pimilingay,* they were *taay.* But since they were also high enough to be able to touch their *pilung*'s food, the comb allowed them to carry it without contaminating it with dirt that might get on their hands from their hair.

Below *milingay ni arow,* the other *pimilingay* villages all performed the services I have described. The differences between them were marked mainly by their varying activities and eating habits. Only the lowest, *milingay ni kan,* would eat moray eels or catch fish with poison, a practice which, perhaps because of its simplicity and efficacy, was considered extremely *taay.* They would also eat shark (*ayong*), stingray (*rol*), and squid (*k'ay*), which, like eel (*luwoth*), were all considered *taay,* though not quite as strongly, since people of *yagug* and *milingay* villages might also eat them. It was admitted

that *pilung* villagers might eat these things, too—except eel—if they
liked the taste, though they would not do so openly. Some *milingay
ni kan* were said even to eat rats, since they lived far from the sea and
had no fish. The story was told of how they would pile rocks together
and then sprinkle them with grated coconut. When the pile became
infested with rats, they would throw a net over it and then crush the
rats between the rocks. This particular practice was attributed to
only one village, but it makes the position of the *pimilingay* quite
clear.

Even though any particular person born to one of the *pimilingay*
ranks was essentially limited to that sphere throughout life, individ-
ually forever *taay* and unable to become *tabugul,* there was still seen
to be a possibility of a kind of advancement up through these
different ranks, similar to the advancement in the estate and the
village. This could occur specifically through the out-marrying of
clan women who each generation would come to possess new land
for their clan "people." What one woman and her children did
within one estate, successive women could do for their clan line
through a series of estates. *Pimilingay* clan lines, or anyone else,
could, through successive generations of women, move up through
the ranks, it was said, marrying from one level of estate and village
to the next, until they eventually married into the highest *pilung*
estate of the highest village. This was perfectly acceptable. No one,
or no one clan "people" belonged inherently at any one level, but all
participated in the process of development of the fundamental dialectic. The proper course for all things on Yap, one man remarked,
was to seek a higher level.

There was finally one further position that was considered the
most *tabugul* of all, higher than the *munthing* level of the *yogum.*
That was the high priest, the *peteliu.* He was the keeper of the shrine
(*teliu*) that belonged to one of the seven spirits, *kan,* that were
responsible for all life on Yap, for the fertility of the land, the
fertility of the people, and all natural occurrences. Very little was
remembered about these seven spirits (Magorgoy, Abrig, Wuthirey,
Ath, Tem'ir, Ngul, Yangalob) or the ritual practices dedicated to
them, but it was clear that they played an important role in the
traditional culture. The *peteliu* was identified with the *kan,* "speaking the *kan*'s voice" (*be a kan u lugun*). The land from which he ate
was the most *tabugul* on Yap, being part of the *kan*'s shrine. It would
be worked not by his wife but by another man specifically designated
to take care of his food and cook for him. Nor could the *peteliu* eat

food from other land or even have his own food cooked elsewhere. His activities were strictly limited. He lived secluded from most people and could move about only on religious business, performing the yearly cycle of rituals in the different high villages. Like the *tabugul* man of the estate or the *tabugul* chief of the village, the *peteliu* was supported by those over whom he had authority. The *peteliu* could not go fishing and depended on the *pilung* to provide for him. In that sense, he could maintain his seclusion and do the *kan*'s work only as the whole system of social relations beneath him functioned. He depended on the authority of the paramount chiefs, which was dependent upon that of the lesser chiefs, as they depended in turn on the men of the estate.

The *peteliu*'s power came from the *kan,* for whom he spoke; it was through that relation that he could perform the rituals that would bring food and prosperity, as well as the rituals that could bring destruction and death to people through typhoons, illness, famine, or misfortune. Neither the *kan* nor the *peteliu* acted alone in this. The paramount chiefs of Yap would advise the *peteliu* of the general state of affairs, whether the people were following established custom or abusing the land, or of the relations between people, and the *peteliu* would supplicate the *kan* to either reward or punish them. If the chiefs saw that people were abusing the resources of the land and becoming disrespectful to authority, they would instruct the *peteliu* to ask the *kan* to cause a typhoon or a plague or a famine to devastate the people and bring them back in line. The *peteliu* could act in this way only as the chiefs instructed him.

That which would bring about such retributions most certainly, people said, was the general abuse of food. One did not just casually open a coconut, drink it, and throw it away. All parts of it were to be looked after so they could be used—the juice, the husk, the shell, the meat. It would not do for the *pilung* to see coconuts generally thrown about. Similarly, when a person finished eating, he was not to leave food lying about, but was to gather it up and hang it up in a basket. A person who did otherwise would be told that, should the *pilung* see it, they would cause a kind of "famine" (*uyngol*)—then, although people would not lack food, as much as they might eat they would not be full or gather nourishment from it.

The people depended on the fertility the *kan* provided, but the *kan* would provide fertility only as the people earned it, as they abode by those relations which, as we have seen, dealt with the basic interactions of people and land. From the fragmentary accounts of the religious cycles comes the description of a ceremony called the *magath e marfaw,* "the striking of the *marfaw.*" The *peteliu* would prepare special *marfaw,* the hibiscus strands worn by all women after they reached womanhood. The *marfaw* the *peteliu* made differed slightly from those worn by women in that they were wider, with only one strand of hibiscus knotted in front around the neck. The *peteliu* would come to where the men of the top *tabugul* eating classes were gathered and, striking the *marfaw* in an incantation to the *kan,* would pass them out to the men, who would put them on. The rest of the ceremony was simply a distribution of *yogum* food. Very little explanation of the ceremony was given, except that it was to reaffirm the men's allegiance to the *kan* and the *yogum* relations and to make them prosper in the coming year. But the implication was clear: people were to the *kan* as women were to men. As the man provided that which would make the woman's labor productive, so did the *kan* for the people as a whole. As the woman provided that which would make the fertility the man had invested in the land productive, so the people made the *kan's* fertility productive.

In the end, no person was really *tabugul.* As much as one group of people depended on how the previous group had transformed the land, they all ultimately depended on the land's natural fertility. People did work on the land and transform it, giving it fertility, but that fertility was never exactly the same as the fertility of the land itself. The ideology of *tabugul* and *taay* thus expressed the fact that while all people on Yap could be distinguished by the different roles they played in the same fundamental dialectic of land and people, in the end all people in Yapese culture, chiefs as well as villagers, *pilung* as well as *pimilingay,* men as well as women, were *taay*— dependent upon the inherent productivity of nature.

6 "The Side of the Chiefs" vs. "The Side of the Young Men"

Although the exact context of political power and authority in which estates within a village and villages within Yap as a whole came to have different ranks and statuses remains obscure, the rather fragmentary and generalized accounts that were given of Yapese politics do present us with a familiar pattern. The structures of political leadership on Yap were described explicitly in terms of the relationships established within the estate, as structures which in a general sense were based on those relationships. As the working out of the dialectic of clan and estate shaped the organization of authority within the estate, so it appears to have shaped the organization of political authority again and again up through the structure of power, culminating in the relations of the paramount chiefs of Yap.

We will be able to analyze only the broadest constructs of Yapese political authority, the very general traditional notions of politics that still informed Yapese life. People continually stressed, however, that although they did not know most of the details, the prerogatives of traditional leadership had once been very highly defined and specific, restricting what a certain chief could do in what situation, in what way he could do it, and on whom he could count for support. They described a complex political field dominated by strong district chiefs, each poised against the other in intensive status rivalry. Each chief would attempt to manipulate to his own ends the maze of diplomatic channels that connected the different villages, whether for the settlement of grievances, for the participation in competitive intervillage ceremonial exchanges and dances, or for warfare, jealously guarding his own prerogatives against encroachment while at the same time trying to increase his power at the expense of others. The balance between political powers appears to have been rather precarious and constantly in the process of being reformulated, ultimately through warfare and the negotiations realigning alliances surrounding it. A web of tribute relations, apparently of minor economic significance though politically symbolic, testified to the fact that most villages had either gained or lost power at one time or another through the course of Yapese history. The political system, in short, seems to have once been quite highly elaborated, a dynamic system of constant rivalry, intricate diplomacy, and warfare, and it thus must be remembered that what follows is only its most basic framework.

Power within the village was described as being administered mainly by those of three different statuses: the "elder of the village" (*pilibithir ko binaw*), the "chief of the village" (*pilung ko binaw*), and the "chief of the young men" (*pilung ko pagal*), also called the "voice of the young men" (*langan pagal*). While the statuses referred to age differences, they were inherent in separate estates and would be exercised by the men of those estates regardless of their comparative ages. Those who exercised the statuses were said to administer the village together, meeting to discuss matters before action would be taken. Each, however, had a distinct role. The "elder of the village" (*pilibithir ko binaw*) demanded the most respect. He played an important role in the enactment of the yearly cycle of religious rituals, some of them taking place at his estate, and he based his authority on his particular association with the supernatural. His role in village affairs was to sit and listen to what others proposed and to pass judgment on its wisdom, taking care that it would offend neither the spirits not established custom. Were he to reject a proposal, it could not be carried out. The "chief of the village" (*pilung ko binaw*) was next in status. His authority was specifically over the land (*binaw*) and its resources. He provided the strongest leadership in both internal and external village affairs, deciding what projects the village should undertake, whether it was the communal construction of a large taro patch or other improvements within the village, an intervillage exchange, or warfare. The "voice of the young men" (*langan pagal*) was the lowest of the three in status but enjoyed considerable political power. He was the representative of the general population of the village, the "young men" (*pagal*). It was he who would actively lead them in the tasks designated by the "chief" and sanctioned by the village "elder." Whereas the "elder" would sit quietly and only voice his approval or disapproval and the "chief" would direct what was to be done, the "voice of the young men" would get up and see that things were carried out, dispatching people to different tasks.

Were the "chief of the village" to decide that the village should give a ceremony marking the completion of a village building project, for example, he would present the idea to the other chiefs in council, outlining the tasks that would have to be done, the communications with the villages to be included, the preparation of men's or women's dances, the cleaning of the village, and the collection of the necessary valuables and food. It would be up to the "elder of the village" to ensure that the planning and execution of the ceremony followed customary practice and did not breach any of the relations existing with other villages. The "chief of the young men" would be responsible for the actual implementation of the plan, himself carrying word of the ceremony to the other villages involved, allocating work to be done by the different groups within the village, checking back with them to see that it was proceeding properly, and finally collecting whatever goods would accompany the ceremony. During the actual ceremony, the "chief of the village" and the "elder of the village" would sit together and confer, while the "chief of the young men" would be constantly moving between them and the various other participants, supervising the activities and performing the more important distributions of valuables.

The village generally was seen in estate terms. The highest village chief, the "elder," was considered its first settler, its "father," who had subsequently divided up "his" land and created other estates and statuses as the village had grown. The "chief of the village" and the "chief of the young men" were also said to be like "father" (*citamangin*) and "son" (*fak*), and the three chiefly statuses were seen to follow the pattern of authority found within the estate.

There, the situation was described in terms of the line of command in which a son spoke for his father. The oldest male of the estate would be so old, it was said, that he could no longer move about or conduct the estate affairs. He would simply sleep in the main house, being cared for by his children, his son speaking for him. But even his son would have already grown old and would not be capable of much activity. Only when there was some matter of great importance would he go and personally speak for the land. Otherwise he would just sit on the *ban tabugul* side of the porch outside the house and instruct his own son in turn what to do and say in a given situation. It was that son, the youngest of the three men, who most actively spoke for the estate. When some situation arose in which the estate was involved, that son would come and tell his father, who would listen and then turn and tell his own father, the old man within the house—not that he would necessarily respond.

Having told the old man, he would then talk the situation over with his son, decide the appropriate action, and instruct him accordingly. Then he would turn and tell the old man what had been decided. It was up to the youngest of the three to carry out the decision. If the situation allowed, he could tell his own young son to do certain tasks or carry a message or, if necessary, he would instruct the others of the estate of their tasks in what had been planned.

As the oldest man on the estate embodied the established relations that had made the estate what it was, himself being close to becoming one of its ancestral spirits, so the "elder of the village" embodied the established village traditions. As the next oldest man on the estate exercised the land's authority, so the "chief of the village" exercised the authority of the village land. And as the youngest of the three men, himself not possessing the authority of the land, worked to implement estate decisions, so the "chief of the young men" represented the labor power of those who were without authority but who would implement village decisions.

But while the structure of authority within the village fit neatly into the estate pattern, it was also seen in part to reverse it. The "chief of the village" and the "chief of the young men" were thought to be related not only as "father" and "son," but further as "woman" (*pin*) and "man" (*pumoon*). The "chief of the village" was compared to a woman because in exercising his authority by commanding others, "he just sat" (*ka yigi par*) like a woman who remained within the estate. The very strength of the "chief of the village" in "sitting" while others implemented his decisions was seen to have made him dependent on those who carried out his authority. The "chief of the young men" was compared to a man, going about actively representing the estate, and it was his effectiveness and that of the people of the village whom he directly led that would make the village what it was, strengthening or weakening its social position. The "chief of the village" and the "chief of the young men" were thus seen to be ultimately complementary, necessarily balanced against each other for the village to prosper, the one "speaking for" the village's landed authority, expressing the established power it embodied, and the other "speaking for" the village people, representing their concrete strength. It was in this sense that the two chiefs were finally said to be like "siblings" (*wolag*) on an estate, working together and against each other, strengthening the land through their competition. We can diagram the outlines of village leadership, then, as in figure 30, indicating the hierarchical basis of the three chiefly statuses numerically but placing the "chief of the village" and the "chief of the young men" at the same level beneath the "elder of the village."

1. "elder of the village"

2. "chief of the village"   3. "chief of the young men"

Fig. 30. Village leadership

The subdivision of the village into sections and subsections (see map, chap. 1, p. 14) each with its own leaders and each containing estates with specialized statuses that gave it authority over particular religious, economic, or political activities, of course made the structure of village leadership considerably more complex. Estates at all levels were further described as being in constant rivalry, each attempting to maximize its own position and power. The "chief of the village" and the "chief of the young men" encouraged such competition, using it themselves, it was said, to make the village as a whole stronger and more productive as they attempted to maximize its position and power with respect to other villages. But it was this general pattern of estate-based organization that seems to have given village leadership its structure, being also in part repeated in the lower village sections and subsections. And it was this pattern that was reduplicated at the broader levels of intervillage political relations, where its significance for us emerges with greater clarity.

Yapese intervillage political structure was compared to a fishing net (nug) made up of interwoven sections, any organization of villages being called a "section of net" (bayang e nug). The basic form of "net" was the geographical organization of villages into districts. There appear to have been twelve such "nets," most but not all headed by highest-ranking pilung villages: Rumung, Map, Gagil, Tamil, Fanif, Weloy, Rull, Dalipebinaw, Kanfay, Malew, Likaycag, and Gilman (see map 3). The "nets" were considered distinct and separate political entities, aggregations of political power formed around the chiefs of strong local villages, either as they had traditionally held power or as they had gained it through warfare and political maneuvering. The village seems to have remained the fundamental locus of power on Yap, with the leading village or villages in each "net" having set channels of communication (tha') with other villages, by which they could conduct external

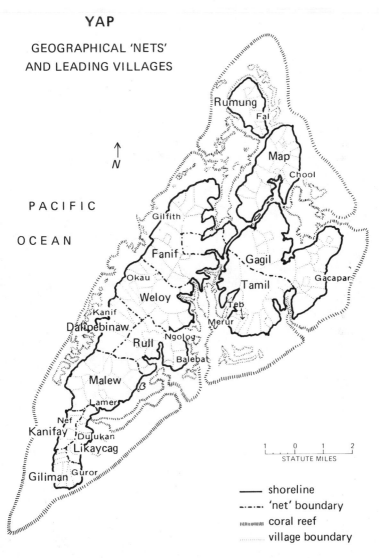

YAP

GEOGRAPHICAL 'NETS' AND LEADING VILLAGES

PACIFIC

OCEAN

Rumung

Fal

Map

Chool

Gilfith

Fanif

Gagil

Okau

Tamil

Gacapar

Weloy

Kanif

Teb

Dalipebinaw

Merur

Ngolog

Rull

Balebat

Malew

Lamer

Nef

Kanifay

Dujukan

Likaycag

Giliman

Guror

| 1 | 0 | 1 | 2 |

STATUTE MILES

—— shoreline

–·–·– 'net' boundary

coral reef

·········· village boundary

Map 3. (Adapted from Lingenfelter 1971.)

political affairs. People would stay close to their own village, travel within Yap being made somewhat hazardous by intervillage political hostility and rivalry. The result seems to have been some degree of isolation of one "net" from another. There were quite distinctive regional differences in dialect as well as purported differences in character, those farther from the centers of Yap-wide political power being generally considered less sophisticated and comparatively uncultured.

Three major centers of political power stood out among these geographical "nets," one in Gagil in northwestern Yap, another in Tamil in central Yap, and a third in Rull in southern Yap. In each of these areas, political leadership was held by a paramount chief's estate that had the status of "elder of the nation" (*pilibithir ko nam*) and a complementary pair of villages or village sections beneath it, one considered *bulce* and the other considered *ulun*: Buluwol estate and Thoolang and Ariap sections of Gacapar village in Gagil, Arib estate and Tab and Merur villages in Tamil, and Ru'way estate and Ngolog and Balebat villages in Rull. The three "elder" estates were *suon* or "overlord" of central, northern, and southern Yap. Each was associated with a sacred place where the people of Yap were thought to have originated or initially settled. They were considered both the "mother" (*citiningin*) and "father" (*citamangin*) of the *ulun* and *bulce* beneath them and of all Yap generally. The *bulce* and *ulun* were said to be their "children," the *bulce* being like an older sibling who had stayed on the family land, while the *ulun* was younger, having moved off and established itself elsewhere. It was the *bulce-ulun* relationship in these three areas that gave the terms their meaning, the other high-ranking villages designated as *bulce* or *ulun*—who formed the main leadership of the district "nets"—being considered such only through their alliance with the top three.

With the paramount "elder" estates, the three *bulce* in Tamil, Rull, and Gagil were considered places of the historic chiefs of Yap. Ngolog in Rull was the place where the first beings were said to have emerged and settled. Tab in Tamil was the place where people reemerged after a flood that was said to have devastated all of Yap. And Gacapar in Gagil was said to be an early area of settlement as well as the place from which the people and land of the nearby atoll of Ulithi were thought to have originated. The *bulce* were thus those who, in an important sense, were the founders of Yapese society. They were *suon* over the land, having had first claim to it, and thereby commanded those who had come to live on it. The strength of the *bulce* was in their land, which gave them power over all others.

The *ulun* were considered to have power not in traditional authority, but in actual might. The *ulun* villages were not traditional centers of power. People in Rull told how the *ulun* village of Balebat was once a small and low village called Mugur. They were not sure exactly how it had become *ulun* but said that its power arose long after that of Ngolog, its neighboring *bulce* village. Balebat was built out onto the tidal flats. The name itself means "trunks of the *bat'* trees." Balebat, they explained, had been built where a stand of *bat'* trees had been cut down and covered with dirt. People in Tamil said that the *ulun* village of Merur was once part of the *bulce* village of Tab, but as sea area had been filled in to accommodate a growing village population it had become a separate village that then assumed power. Information about Ariap section of Gacapar village in Gagil was less detailed, but it was also said to have been settled after the *bulce* section, Thoolang.

Buluwol estate		Arib estate		Ru'way estate	
"elder of the nation"		"elder of the nation"		"elder of the nation"	
Thoolang section— Gacapar village (*bulce*)	Ariap section— Gacapar village (*ulun*)	Tab village (*bulce*)	Merur village (*ulun*)	Ngolog village (*bulce*)	Balebat village (*ulun*)
GAGIL (Northern Yap)		TAMIL (Central Yap)		RULL (Southern Yap)	

Fig. 31. The centers of political power on Yap

All that the *ulun* possessed was considered to have come from the *bulce*. The relation was again like that of "father" to "son" and was described as such. The *ulun* were the "hands" (*bugul i pa'*) of the *bulce*, those who moved about and did the work, while the *bulce* sat and gave orders. The *ulun* were said to do nothing without the knowledge of the *bulce*, acting specifically for them. It was difficult to get people to speak in precise terms, but it did appear that the *ulun* performed those tasks appropriate to "young men," carrying messages, bringing fish, and above all, fighting. It was said that the top *bulce* would not themselves fight wars but would send their "army," the *ulun*. Because the *ulun* were under the authority of the *bulce*, they were considered to be slightly lower in rank, though still of the same general level, and women could marry between *ulun* and *bulce* villages with no real change in status. It was in serving the *bulce* chiefs that the *ulun* were said to have amassed their power. While again precise accounts were lacking, the *ulun* were generally described as having built up a widespread network of villages under their own authority as they traveled about Yap for the *bulce*, eventually gaining the might to equal the *bulce*'s traditional authority.

Together, the estates of the "elder of the nation" and the paired *bulce* and *ulun* beneath them formed the political leadership of northern, central, and southern Yap. As "elders," the paramount chiefs were mainly counselors. They would sit at the head of the regional chief's councils and listen to what was proposed by the *bulce* and *ulun* leaders, watching to see that traditional relations were upheld and respected. The "elders" were considered part of the *bulce* on the side of traditional authority. Yet although they tended to side with the wisdom of the *bulce*, they were equally the "parent" of the *ulun* and had to see that their interests were protected too. In any conflict that arose, the "elder" was said to have the role of peacemaker, intervening as both a "father" with superior authority and a "mother" concerned that her children did not harm themselves.

Each of the *bulce* and *ulun* was also the regional leader of one side of two opposed Yap-wide alliances, groupings of villages of all ranks that were allied politically, the *bulce* heading the "side of the chiefs" (*ban pilung*) and the *ulun* heading the "side of the young men" (*ban pagal*). While much about the alliances remains unclear, they seem to have functioned mainly with respect to intervillage political rivalry and warfare. The two alliances would not fight each other as groups. Rather, by formally allying one village to another under the *bulce* and *ulun*, they seem to have stabilized and limited the scope of conflict. The alliances appear to have created a balanced structure of relations that could allow individual villages already in power to maintain their position, permitting continual minor local readjustments of status and power involving a few villages at a time to take place without causing major political disruptions.

The "side of the chiefs" under the *bulce* was said to be not extensive, encompassing few villages, but to include land that was considered the most powerful on Yap. It was the side of traditional landed authority and power, its *bulce* leaders being characterized as older men, wise, experienced, and having a powerful voice in all affairs. This was said to be reflected even in their personal style. The leading *bulce* would dress conservatively, wearing short combs in their hair, carrying short baskets, and being modest in the way they wore the hibiscus fiber belt that marked manhood. The more extensive "side of the young men" was seen as the side of newly arisen might, its *ulun* leaders being characterized, in contrast to the *bulce,* as young men, strong and active though not overly wise. As befitting young men, they were said to go about with something of a swagger, wearing long, decorated combs in their hair, carrying long, outsized baskets, and wearing billows of hibiscus fiber. Heading the "side of the chiefs," the *bulce* were reserved and would never reveal what they were thinking; heading the "side of the young men," the *ulun* were impetuous, always ready for a fight.

The actual functioning of these alliances will become clearer when we discuss the Yap-wide political organization. Here, however, it is important to note the structural change that seems to have taken place as the estatelike pattern of authority was raised to the level of regional authority. The underlying structure of relations between the paramount "elder of the nation" estate and the *bulce/ban pilung* and *ulun/ban pagal* beneath them was clearly the same as that of the relations of the leading statuses of the village, the "elder of the village," the "chief of the village," and the "voice of the young men," which reduplicated, as we saw, the hierarchical structure of authority within the estate (see fig. 32).

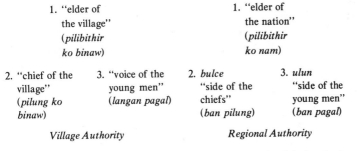

	1. "elder of the village" (*pilibithir ko binaw*)		1. "elder of the nation" (*pilibithir ko nam*)	
2. "chief of the village" (*pilung ko binaw*)		3. "voice of the young men" (*langan pagal*)	2. *bulce* "side of the chiefs" (*ban pilung*)	3. *ulun* "side of the young men" (*ban pagal*)
	Village Authority		*Regional Authority*	

Fig. 32. The symmetrical structure of village and regional political authority

But again, the relation between the *bulce* and *ulun* was also significantly different from the estate pattern. The *bulce* and *ulun* were seen as complementary, having different though equal power, as should already be evident from the description of the two alliances they headed. The word *bulce* itself denoted a side house beam that carried the main weight of a building, while the word *ulun* denoted an extremely tall tree, one which had grown up above the rest. Such *ulun* trees were considered particularly strong and were used in making certain medicines. The *bulce* house beams, it was said, were strong and sturdy, the strength of the building, never moving. The *ulun* trees were strong but, being too high, tended to be blown one way then another by the winds.

The *bulce* and *ulun* were also considered to follow the pattern of both "father" and "son" and "man" and "woman," the *bulce* being the source of the *ulun*'s power, as "father" to "son," but at the same time "just sitting" like "women" at the historic centers of power, while the *ulun*, like "men," went about actively trying to improve their social position and establish themselves in the social world. In serving the *bulce* chiefs, the *ulun* were said to have become the aggressive force in Yapese politics, not simply the "army" of the *bulce,* but themselves a powerful faction, not simply the messengers of the *bulce,* but the leaders of an alliance with extensive ties with other villages. This characterization of *bulce* as "women" and *ulun* as "men" was reinforced by the fact that the *bulce* were considered *suon* of the land and what it produced, while the *ulun,* said to possess few land resources, were considered *suon* of the sea, having become more attached to it, traveling about on it by canoe, and depending on its resources. People told of competitive exchanges in which the *bulce,* being like "women" and *suon* of the land, would give garden food, while the *ulun,* being like "men" and *suon* of the sea, would give fish.

Significantly, the estate status characterizations applied to the *bulce-ulun* relationship here seem to present an unfolding dynamic between them. The "father"-"son" historic relationship by which the *ulun* were said to have derived their powers from the *bulce* was seen to have specifically produced the opposing relationship of "woman"-"man." With the continuing growth of the younger *ulun* villages, the *ulun* had become significant aggregations of new power that could actively oppose the established landed *bulce,* delineating their power (as "man" to "woman") as much as the *bulce* had delineated the power of the *ulun* (as "father" to "son"). As opposing equal forces, the *bulce* and *ulun* and the two alliances under them were thus finally considered also to be "siblings" (*wolag*), conflict between them again being the competition of brothers who worked together and against each other on the same estate.

This dynamic reemerges as the pattern of modified estate relations repeats itself at last at the highest level of Yapese politics in the relations between the three centers of political power themselves in Tamil, Rull, and Gagil. Tamil—Arib estate and Tab (*bulce*) and Merur (*ulun*) villages—was considered the "elder" of all Yap, the paramount *pilibithir ko nam*. It was in Tamil that present-day Yap was thought to have originated. The story was told of a flood that was brought down on Yap by a spirit. All the people were killed except the spirit's daughter, Labirang, and her husband, Rigog, who built a tower in Tamil to escape from the waters, and one other man who survived on a raft. It was from Labirang and Rigog and their seven spirit children (Magorgoy, Abirg, Wuthirey, Ath, Tem'ir, Ngul, and Yangalob) that Yapese culture was reestablished in Tamil. Several of the most important shrines on Yap were there and were said to contain relics from the events surrounding the flood. The shrines were associated with Arib estate, and its holder would play an important part in the religious rituals commemorating aspects of the flood story. As the Yap-wide "elder," Tamil had authority over both the political alliances—the "side of the chiefs" and the "side of the young men." Its role again was said to be that of a wise counselor, sitting and listening to what was proposed and giving advice. Tamil, the villages of Tab and Merur, would not themselves fight in wars, at least not under their own banner; the young men of those villages who wanted to fight would join with other forces.

Rull—Ru'way estate and the *bulce* and *ulun* villages of Ngolog and Balebat beneath it—was considered the Yap-wide leader of the "side of the chiefs," *ban pilung*. Rull was also a historic center of Yap and a place of the historic chiefs. It was there that the first beings on Yap were said to have emerged from the land, and there was an important shrine in Rull that was said to contain their place of emergence. Power was seen to have shifted from Rull to Tamil, however, as is indicated by the flood story and the reemergence of people from Tamil. Allied under Rull on the "side of the chiefs" were seven *bulce* villages, the three main *bulce*, Tab, Ngolog, and Thoolang section of Gacapar, plus four others. While people insisted that there were only seven *bulce*, the villages they assigned to the lesser four would vary. They commonly mentioned Gilfith (Fanif), Kanif (Dalipebinaw), N'ef (Kanfay), and Guror (Gilman). Beneath the seven *bulce* were allied villages of all ranks, in all parts of Yap. The villages of *ban pilung* allied under Rull formed one of two major "sections of net" in Yapese politics, and the villages of *ban pagal* allied under Gagil formed the other.

Gagil—Buluwol estate and beneath it the Thoolang (*bulce*) and Ariap (*ulun*) sections of Gacapar—was considered the Yap-wide leader of the "side of the young men," *ban pagal*. Gagil was less a historic center of Yap and more a power that had grown strong through the tribute it received as head of a chain of relations running through the Carolines from island to island almost as far east as Truk. Tribute, moving from one island group to the next, would come to Yap from Ulithi atoll, situated to the northeast of Yap. The relations of the Yapese in Gagil to the Ulithians were much like that of the *pilung* and *pimilingay* in the village rank system. The Yapese were considered to be *suon* of Ulithi, the atoll itself being thought to have been created and populated by Yapese spirit-ancestors. Specific estates on Yap had rights over specific land on Ulithi, the relationship being put in "parent-child" terms. The Ulithians would bring tribute to Yap, such as woven mats or cloth, coconut-husk rope important in building and canoe construction, coconut oil, or candy, and receive in return wood for building canoes, food, flint, tumeric, and other items scarce in the atolls.[1] This relationship with Ulithi and the islands to the east appears to have given Gagil considerable strength. People never failed to associate the power of Gagil with its position with respect to the eastern islands. The chiefs of Gagil were said to have used the distribution of the articles received as tribute, all of which were highly prized on Yap, as a means of establishing and maintaining political alliances. According to Lingenfelter (1971), the power of Gagil became so strong as a consequence that Tamil, which had traditionally remained neutral between *ban pilung* and *ban pagal*, came to side with Rull as *ban pilung* in order to maintain the balance of power.

The *ban pagal* alliance headed by Gagil was indeed said to be much more extensive than the alliance headed by Rull. In opposition to the seven *bulce* of the *ban pilung* were seven *ulun* villages of *ban pagal*, again the three main *ulun*, Merur, Ariap section of Gacapar, and Balebat, plus four others, commonly Cool (Map), Bugol (Tamil), Okau (Weloy), and Anoth (Gilman). Beneath these seven was said to be a large alliance of villages of all ranks that was numerically much superior to *ban pilung*. Just as the *ulun* villages were said to be strong not from the authority of their land but through their extensive allies, so it was with the *ban pagal*.

With Tamil as the "elder of the nation" mediating between the alliance of the "chiefs" and the alliance of the "young men," the structure of Yap-wide political organization reduplicated the pattern of relations in each of the regional centers of power, as the Yapese themselves pointed out (fig. 33). The same characteristics that were described for the *bulce/ban pilung* and *ulun/ban pagal* regionally were also applied at this level with the *ban pilung–ban pagal* relation of Rull and Gagil, which was again like that of "father" to "son," "woman" to "man," and "sibling" to "sibling." Tamil was definitely the founder of the present social order and Gagil a relatively new power that had grown up to challenge the authority of the established chiefs, producing again at the highest level of Yapese social relations a situation where the hierarchical estatelike relations were seen to have developed into a complementary opposition between "chiefs" and "young men."

1. *TAMIL*

Arib
estate

2. Tab	3. Merur
village	village
(*bulce*)	(*ulun*)

"ELDER OF THE NATION"
(*PILIBITHIR KO NAM*)

2. *RULL*   3. *GAGIL*

1. Ru'way estate   1. Buluwol estate

2. Ngolog	3. Balebat	2. Thoolang	3. Ariap
village	village	section*	section*
(*bulce*)	(*ulun*)	(*bulce*)	(*ulun*)

"SIDE OF THE CHIEFS"   "SIDE OF THE YOUNG MEN"
(*BAN PILUNG*)   (*BAN PAGAL*)

*Gacapar village

Fig. 33. The pattern of Yapese political authority

Together, these three groups of *pilibithir* estates and paired *bulce-ulun* villages beneath them were seen as fundamental to the stability and prosperity of Yap. They were said to be like three *ngucol,* the three rocks that support a pot over the fire. For the pot to remain upright, they all had to have equal strength. If one were weak in relation to the others, the pot would fall over. This balance was maintained through the functioning of the two war alliances, the "side of the chiefs" and the "side of the young men." Tamil could of course play Rull and Gagil off against each other, keeping their power in balance and also maintaining its own paramount position. But the cross-cutting ties of the *bulce* and *ulun* within the alliances were further said to contribute to stability. Although Rull as a whole was the head of the "side of the chiefs" and Gagil the head of the "side of the young men," the village of Balebat in Rull was *ulun* and had ties with the "side of the young men," and the Thoolang section of Gacapar village in Gagil was *bulce* and had ties with the "side of the chiefs." Tamil likewise had ties to both alliances, the village of Tab being *bulce* and the village of Merur *ulun*. In such a context, political conflict and especially warfare had become as much an exercise in manipulating the complex ties between villages as a show of force.

There were several forms of fighting on Yap. The smallest was said to be fights over women and was called "voice of the children" (*lungun e tir*) or "voice of the handsome men" (*lungun e choay*), "children" because it did not involve the chiefs but merely those under them, their "children." These fights resulted when one man stole another's wife or attempted to do so. The most common goal was for one of the men involved to cut off the other's hair, marking him as disgraced, though it could extend to fights between estates of different villages and perhaps the burning of one of their houses. There were also fights involving revenge for murder (*folebey*) and conflicts over land. These sorts of conflicts could remain at the level of those involved or could be appealed to the chiefs for their intervention.

Warfare, however, was described as having required the utmost political skill of the chiefs. It was through warfare that the chiefs at all levels attempted to maintain and improve their positions. In carrying on a war, a chief had to think above all of the structure of power relations in which he was involved. Were he to go beyond his own prerogatives and appear too politically aggressive and a threat to the overall balance of power, then steps would inevitably be taken against him. Wars were described as limited engagements fought at designated battle areas (*tethil*) inland or on the tidal flats and involving few combatants, most often close or neighboring villages of opposite alliances who had a history of hostility and rivalry, along with a few of their allies. Secret communications and countercommunications between chiefs at all levels were said to arrange the outcome of a war before it was fought, realigning alliances into a new, generally acceptable configuration and deciding who would be killed, how much damage would be done, and who would emerge victorious. The two sides would meet at a war ground and fight until the goal had been achieved, usually the death of a chief or a dangerously skilled fighter or the burning of a man's house. Other people might be wounded, but the strongest and most expert fighters, warriors specialized in the martial arts, would have been told by the chiefs whom to kill and would duly liquidate them. Once the objective of the fight had been achieved, it was said, the proper steps would be taken and the war halted. Even in such a prearranged war, however, no one could be absolutely certain of the outcome, since those who had thought themselves in on the plotting of it could easily find themselves tricked into being the actual victims, if other more powerful chiefs within the alliances had secretly communicated against them. The exercise of warfare was unanimously said to be the most difficult endeavor on Yap, a morass of tricks and shifting alliances in which success required great skill and knowledge.

There were numerous stories of the wars on Yap. The following, recorded by Schneider in 1947–48 and concerning an attack on Fal village in Rumung, gives some idea of the nature of warfare and of the ways the various cross-cutting ties between villages were used and created:

> Long ago Rumung only helped Gatchepar in case of war. But once the people of Kanif came and burned down the *p'ebai* (community center) of Fal and killed some people. Word went to Gatchepar of what happened. Gatchepar came to Rumung and, at the same time, sent word to Gilfith. The chief of Gatchepar, Fonepuluw, was of the same family as Waath, the chief of Gilfith.
>
> The chiefs of Gatchepar and Gilfith came to Rumung and conferred. Thipongeg was the chief of Kanif at the time. When he had heard what the people of Kanif had done, Waath said, "This is not good. Where is Thipongeg now?" The Rumung people said he was at Becheyel village on Map. Waath said that he would go to see him. The *p'ebai* was still smouldering. They took a smouldering piece of the *p'ebai* with them.
>
> So they took all the men they could, and one burning brand from the *p'ebai* and the people of Gilfith went to Map in canoes. They anchored their canoes near Amin village. Then they went

to fight. Waath and another person went inland a ways, and this other person was sent to call Thipongeg to fight.

Thipongeg wore a red hibiscus shirt called *ligow*. He was seen coming, because of this red shirt, before he saw many people were waiting for him. When he did see them waiting, he ran into the sea.

When Waath saw Thipongeg coming, he took a rope which was tied to the float of a canoe by mistake. He tied this rope about his waist as a war decoration. And he ran, forgetting to cut the rope free of the float. He tripped, pulling the float around sharply and almost breaking it from the outrigger struts. Then he cut the rope and ran to fight.

Waath had brought seven men with him. Thipongeg was alone, so he ran away. They chased him into the village and onto the hills behind the village. They chased him a long time. When Thipongeg ran to the hills, he tried to climb the retaining wall of a garden by grasping a bush over his head, but it tore out by the roots and he fell back down.

As he had climbed the wall, Waath and his seven men were close behind him and when he tried to climb the wall, they were all underneath him. When he grasped the bush and the bush gave way, he fell back on top of their upturned split bamboo spears and died.

They put his body on a canoe and brought it to Fal.

Waath said to the chief of Gatchepar, "Here is the man. He is killed." So the two conferred. They conferred about whether to bring the body to Gatchepar or Gilfith. They decided that they couldn't bring it to Gilfith because Gilfith is *ban pilung* and Thipongeg was from a *ban pilung* village, too. So they took it to Gatchepar. Properly, Thipongeg and Waath should not have fought, being both on the same allied side; but in this case Waath was acting for his family, not his village, so it was all right.

So Waath said to the Gatchepar chief, because they were both of the same *tabinaw*, "give me something of Rumung for this." So the chief of Gatchepar said, "Take the food for a *togumog* (religious celebration requiring bananas, coconuts, and fish) and the rights to the *tongir* fish." But Waath said, "No, there is something yet." The Gatchepar chief said, "What?" And Waath said, "Spears." The Gatchepar chief said, "No, you cannot have them all. One is for you and one is for me." Waath said, "That is good."

Since then all the *tongir* fish caught go to Gilfith, and whenever Gilfith wants food for a *togumog*, Rumung supplies them, and when Gilfith has a war, then Rumung sends men to help them.

It was out of such events that villages could gain or lose in power. The village of Gilfith, for example, was said to have once been a lower village that slowly established ties with other villages, amassing considerable power and finally being taken into the ranks of the *bulce*. Gilfith was also said to have had almost no high-ranking taro patches even after it became *bulce* and got them only by annexing them in a war with the neighboring village of Rutnu, then an *ulun* village.

Yet while a chief could gain in power through warfare, even raising the rank of his village, he could do so only through the most careful political maneuvering, readjusting power relations to his own advantage only on the pretext of maintaining the existing balance and without appearing so aggressive as to invite reprisal. Warfare and conflict on Yap were explicitly described as readjusting the balance between groups, most generally between the "side of the chiefs" and the "side of the young men." The two alliances were said to be "two sides of a stone fish trap" (*braba' e atch nge braba'*). The stone fish trap (*atch*) was a long stone wall running out to sea and ending in an arrowhead-shaped enclosure that would trap the fish as the tide receded. One side fit symmetrically with the other. Neither side could gain by trying to obliterate the other in a war of all against all. Such a war, people said, would have been disastrous. Everything would have been destroyed and no one would have won.

Warfare was to maintain a balance within the given structure of political relations and therefore was not to end with one side having excessively reduced the other. A parablelike story was told in this respect. A war was fought between birds from the north end of Yap and birds from the south end. One side routed the other, which flew away in retreat. But one of their number, a bird with little endurance (*chowigil*) had landed and got the tips of its wings stuck in the mud (which is why this species has dark-tipped wings on its light body). Realizing their companion was in trouble, the defeated birds returned and routed the birds of the other side. The point of the story was said to be that you should watch out what you did to the other side, because they would inevitably return and do it to you.

In general outline, then, the Yapese political system described a process by which estate relations were raised to increasingly higher levels of social interaction through the development of the villages and village power, ultimately producing a new set of opposing political relationships and thereby creating the Yap-wide balanced opposition of the two alliances. The alliances themselves, as well as the *bulce-ulun* relations within them and the relations of village authority, were all specifically seen as the products of a process of political development, being described in essentially historical terms. Although it is now impossible to know the precise history that lay behind those terms, the kind of development they describe does make sense, especially in the context of the dialectic of clan and estate we have found to be central to Yapese culture.

The fact that each of the regional "elder" estates was considered to be part of one of the *bulce-ulun* pairs, that in one case the *bulce-ulun* pair were part of the same village, Gacapar, that in another case the pair was said to have been historically one village, Tab, and that in the third case Ngolog and Balebat were neighboring villages does suggest a plausible kind of history. The "elder"-*bulce-ulun* organization could have emerged out of the organization of single villages as the population grew and more estates were created through the continual resubdivision of land among sons. If the village split into new villages or village sections under the existing chiefs ("elder of the village," "chief of the village," and "voice of the young men") then the regional leadership pattern would be created. Likewise, the organization of the villages themselves could have emerged earlier out of the estates of the original village founders. Following the political ideology even further, it is not difficult to conceive that this same process would have not only extended estate relations, but also created new aggregations of power in village sections and villages that could have come to challenge the established landed authority from which they had been historically derived. Thus, just as an earlier established clan organization appears to have been adapted into the estate system, so the estate system itself would have become the established order whose own development then led to the creation of new conditions to which it, in turn, was forced to adapt.

The political system seems in some degree to reflect this entire process, the shift from the earlier clan organization, as well as the changes within the developing estate system. For, significantly, the three "elder of the nation" estates of Arib, Ru'way, and Buluwol, which represented the three major areas of Yap, were considered to be "clan land" (*tafen e ganong*), appearing to have retained an earlier clan identity longer than other estates because of their paramount political position. Two of the estates could be held only by members of a specific clan—Buluwol estate in Gagil by members of Weloy clan and Arib estate in Tamil by members of the Fanif clan. The situation with Ru'way estate in Rull was not exactly clear. As far as was remembered, it had been passed not along clan lines but to brothers and children, although the genealogy for the estate itself was not very deep. The current holder said that although it was not passed within the clan, the "voice" of Ru'way belonged to the Ngolog clan and other people just spoke for it. Thus, he explained, it was essentially like the other two "elder" estates.

Succession to the "elder" estates was through the appointment by the chiefs of the *ulun* and *bulce* paired beneath them. At Arib and Buluwol, the chiefs would pick a member of the Fanif and Weloy clan respectively. This gave the chiefs considerable control over the "elder's" authority. It was said that in recent history the chiefs of Tamil had put a Fanif man from a lower-ranking village at Arib in order to ensure their power over it. The fact that Ru'way estate in Rull was said to be land of the Ngolog clan, though not passed along clan lines, may be a result of the Rull chiefs' simply taking control over its authority, subordinating the role of the clan as it had been subordinated in the estates generally.

With this, the political system can broadly be seen to document the changes in Yapese society that took place with the progress of the dialectic we originally identified in the interaction of clan and estate. It was the expression of the constantly changing concrete organizations of power that were formed and transformed as people and land adapted and readapted to each other, as the clan system was shaped into the estate system and the estate system was reshaped by the rise of new village powers and the alliances. As each form of social organization produced its own form of political power, the political system placed the social formations arising specifically out of the dialectic of clan and estate at the center of a historical process, as but one set of historically derived social relations that created—at the same time that they themselves came into being— the conditions for yet other entirely new social forms. In effect, it seems to work out the dialectic of clan and estate at the level of political power and authority, in the conflicts of those groups that arose and competed for control in the historical development of Yapese society.

7 Epilogue

All social life is essentially *practical.* All mysteries which lead
theory to mysticism find their rational solution in human practice
and the comprehension of this practice.

Karl Marx, "7th Thesis on Feuerbach"

We began our study of Yapese traditional ideology by examining
the related constructs of clan (*ganong*) and estate (*tabinaw*), initially
generalizing them into their broadest possible meaning—a dialectic
between people and land—and then suggesting that the two social
forms were related historically as well, reflecting as historical
constructs that same interaction of people and land. Having
proceeded to broaden our description of Yapese culture, we can now
take that historical argument a step further, considering it more
fully and in greater detail. In so doing, we can also begin to look at
the other aspects of Yapese culture historically, trying to perceive
exactly why they had the particular form they did. It is here that the
kind of close cultural analysis we have been attempting should pay
off. For the more accurately and completely we are able to describe
the statements of Yapese culture, the more we should be able to
comprehend those statements in their fundamental reality—that is,
as historical statements made by human actors within the necessities
of a specific social and material context. Even though any account of
"Yapese history" must by necessity remain speculative, it is possible,
I think, to perceive in the traditional ideology the broadest outlines
of just such a context.

At the end of chapter 2 I argued that the clan on Yap could be
seen as a historical matrilineal group that had been adapted to the
particular productive relations of the estate. The social relationship
of the clan seems to have existed before and have defined the
internal estate relations, the transaction of the estate taking place in
terms of the different estate members' previously given clan affiliations. This suggests that Yap was once predominantly a matrilineally organized society, having corporate clan groups such as were
found elsewhere in Micronesia, but which had subsequently been
modified to form the traditional patterns we have described. We
have yet, however, to answer the question of how such a transformation could have occurred.

The answer here seems to lie within the actual process of estate transaction. The process by which one clan group transferred land to another clan group in return for specified services appears as the very means through which the transformation of an earlier matrilineal organization took place, generating not only the estate relations but, as we shall see, the other basic structural features of Yapese traditional culture.

In a society with matrilineal clans and matrilocal residence, women remain on their own clan's land and, assuming clan exogamy, take in husbands from unrelated clan groups. A couple lives "matrilocally" on land belonging to the woman and her parents— land that will be passed to the couple's children as members of the woman's clan. The "clan land," which is commonly identified as such, is thus held continuously by the same matrilineally related group, as is any "clan status." Authority over the matrilineal group and its resources usually remains with the clan men, even though they have moved off the clan land and married elsewhere.

Looked at on a rather mechanistic level, the structure of the Yapese estate system becomes immediately comprehensible as merely a modification of this pattern. For the pattern of estate relations to be produced, one matrilineal and originally matrilocal clan group could have simply subdivided its "clan land" in order to take another unrelated clan group under its authority. This could have occurred when—for whatever reason—the man of a clan remained on his natal clan land instead of marrying out and brought in his wife from another clan, forming what might be seen, as a first approximation, as a kind of "client" relationship with her. The woman who married in would receive a section of land for her own use, land that was to belong specifically to her and her children— perhaps allowing them in that sense to continue to live "matrilocally" on land that had become their own "clan land," as shown diagrammatically in figure 34. In return for the land, the woman and her children would place themselves under the authority of the husband and his clan group, working for them and giving them their allegiance. It was this arrangement, too, that could have provided the basis for the strict separation of food resources around the notions of *tabugul* and *taay*, as I shall argue in detail below, the land-giving clan group and the land they retained for their own use being considered *tabugul*, while the land-receiving clan group and the land they were given for their use were considered *taay*. In order to visualize the estate system as a transformation of an earlier

Yapese matrilineal society, we now need only think of the once-unified clan land of a single matrilineal estate being repeatedly subdivided and transacted between clan groups. As sons repeated what their fathers had done, the estate would ultimately come to accommodate a succession of "client" clan groups, each possessing their own separate "clan land" and each working for their predecessors (fig. 35). As each clan group received land to live from within the estate, each could thus at once continue and extend the matrilineal pattern, still living and raising children "matrilocally" on their "own" land, while at the same time establishing new social patterns, that of the transacted estate and the *tabugul/taay* ranks.

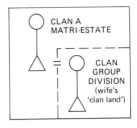

Fig. 34. Division of the matri-estate

While this accounts structurally for the notions of both the transaction of the estate between clan groups and the subdivision of the estate into hierarchically ranked parcels, as indicated, it does not provide the answer to the much more difficult questions—why this transformation of matrilineal organization would have occurred, what its motivations were, or what purpose it served. Here again, however, by looking closely at the estate relations involved, their content as well as their form, we can, I think, pose at least a tentative answer.

We can begin by noting that both the transaction and the hierarchical subdivision of the estate functioned not in terms of land generally, *but predominantly in terms of taro-producing land,* or the taro patch (*muut*). Taro was the basic staple of the Yapese diet, and it was specifically access to different-ranking taro patches within the estate that marked its members' differential estate rank. It was also the possession of a ranking taro patch that defined a person's ability to enter a particular village *yogum* rank, since only those men who held the highest-ranking *munthing* taro patches were able to enter

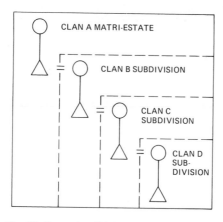

Fig. 35. Successive divisions of the matri-estate

the *munthing* rank. But what is there about taro production that makes this seem significant?

In his comparative study of cultural adaptation in the Carolines, Alkire (1960) found that among the eight island groups he analyzed (high islands: Palau, Yap, Truk, Palau; low atolls: Ulithi, Ifaluk, Losap, Mokil) taro cultivation as a single primary crop tended consistently to be correlated with patrilocal residence and patrilineal inheritance; that is, a pattern like that on Yap, where a man and his wife live with or near the man's parents and where property is passed from father to son. He identified two extreme socioeconomic formations within the Carolines representative of possible historical stages:

> (1) a homestead group depending on dispersed and/or multiple-crop agriculture and following matrilineal inheritance and matri-local residence rules; and
> (2) a concentrated village group with centralized and/or single-crop economy together with patrilocal residence and patrilineal inheritance. [Alkire 1960, p. 147]

Alkire suggests that settlement patterns "tend to be ecologically adjusted to the agricultural crops." The Carolinian cultures dependent upon a diversified agricultural base, including crops requiring different kinds of growing areas that can be distributed throughout an island in hillside gardens, taro patches, and breadfruit groves, tend toward a dispersed homestead settlement pattern. Those cultures dependent on a primary-crop agricultural base of taro, a crop extremely restricted in its growing area, similarly tend toward a more compact village settlement pattern. Alkire also suggests that the different labor requirements of these two forms of agriculture could further account for the shift in residence and inheritance from the first formation to the second that seems to have occurred in some places:

> The Caroline Islands have a tradition of matrilineality. Historically, the people may have entered the area with a matrilineal organization or have developed it following settlement of some island of the group and before moving on to others. Matrilineality today seems to be a tradition which is mainly associated with a pattern of homesteads and dispersed farming. In these areas of dispersed agriculture the large extended family unit is well suited to work the land profitably. Historically, this organization was most likely accompanied throughout the Carolines by a matrilocal family unit which provided sufficient labour to work the land belonging to a matrilineage. Carolinian areas of dispersed homestead settlement do have matrilocal patterns which correspond with the tradition of matrilineality. In those island groups which developed a settlement pattern associated with more centralized resources and population concentration the extended family would not be needed to work the land. In such instances the garden area was either close at hand or, if at some distance, still of an undiversified nature, and a smaller family unit could profitably work it. Under such conditions a variation in family composition in relation to the residence unit could more easily occur. In areas of concentrated settlement in the Carolines residence rules often vary from the matrilocal tradition, and in some cases only a remnant of the original matrilineality remains. [Alkire 1960, pp. 146–47]

Since it is probable that taro cultivation was originally not a primary mode of food production on Yap, the fact that the patrilocal and "patrilineal"[1] estate system was explicitly organized around taro production thus seems to suggest that the shift from an earlier matrilineal/matrilocal organization was indeed linked to a shift in agricultural practice.

Although taro cultivation was most likely always known to the Yapese, Barrau suggests it came to predominate in the South Pacific only with the decreasing viability of shifting agriculture—or what is variously termed swidden agriculture, slash-and-burn agriculture, or field-forest rotation—for supporting an increasing population:

> It is probable that the original agricultural systems, at least on
> the high islands, were either shifting agriculture or agriculture
> with bush-fallowing rotation. Burning was used for clearing
> space for gardens. Increased populations and the use of primitive
> agricultural techniques were probably responsible for deteriora-
> tion of both vegetation and soils on the majority of high islands.
> With the decrease in land fertility it became necessary to employ
> semi-permanent forms of agriculture with artificial fertilization
> of the soil. It was this need, apparently, that led to the
> development of taro growing on low-lying, hydromorphic soils
> and on irrigated terraces in the villages. [Alkire 1960, p. 18]

The role of shifting hillside gardens (*milay'*) in traditional Yapese
agriculture makes this seem quite plausible. They supplemented
the daily diet mainly with yams, of which the Yapese distinguished
more than thirty varieties (Defngin 1959), some also having important prestige value in certain ceremonial offerings. Various melons,
sugarcane, and sweet potatoes were commonly intercropped
between the yam mounds, providing further variety to the diet.
Only the poorer *pimilingay* groups living inland were said to have
traditionally relied on the gardens as their main source of subsistence. But it is clear that Yap's hillside forests could have once
allowed the fairly extensive development of an entire society based
predominantly on shifting agriculture.

Following Alkire, it does not seem unreasonable to see that
society as matrilineal and matrilocal. Assuming a division of labor
similar to that later found on Yap, the women gardening and the
men fishing, early shifting agriculture would have certainly been
quite amenable to matrilineality and matrilocality, contributing to
its maintenance if not its development. Shifting cultivation involves
clearing a plot of land by cutting back and burning the forest
cover, then farming the ash-enriched garden for one or more years,
after which the land is allowed to lie fallow and return to bush
before being reused. The labor requirements of repeatedly clearing
dispersed garden plots would favor cooperative work such as could
be easily accomplished by the related women of a matrilineage
living together with their in-marrying husbands on a joint estate.
We still saw women helping each other in clearing their hillside
gardens by forming mutual-aid groups, though now they are
usually made up of affinal relatives or close friends.

Yet in that the practice of shifting agriculture was associated
with the earlier matrilineal forms, it would also have set limits to

them. One of the most important characteristics of shifting agriculture is the absolute natural limitation of its productivity owing to the necessity of letting the land recuperate during a fallow period. As has been most vividly described by Geertz (1968, pp. 20–25) in his review of shifting agriculture, the practice essentially involves a "canny imitation" of the dynamics of the natural ecosystem into which it is projected, the dense tropical forest flourishing on the usually impoverished, leached tropical soils. Forest growth in this setting normally maintains itself by constantly recycling the dead organic matter that accumulates and quickly decomposes on the forest floor; slash-and-burn farming simply accelerates and directs this process, speeding the decomposition through burning and using the collected nutrients on the soil's surface to support food cuitivation. The slash-and-burn process, however, is less efficient than the natural self-sustaining cycle, both because of the large amount of energy lost in the burning process and because the cultivated plants, being less pulpy, cannot return the same amount of nutrients to the soil as does the forest growth. The plot thus quickly becomes less productive and must be left fallow to restore itself. If the plot is not cultivated too long and is allowed to remain fallow long enough, a balanced and productive farming cycle can be sustained, in spite of the generally impoverished soil conditions. To overuse the land, however, can lead to an irreversible process of ecological deterioration. The plots become unable to recover, and forest growth is replaced by savanna grass (*imperata*), signaling the end of the land's usefulness for reburning and cultivation. In many parts of the upland area of Yap, one could see old garden sites that had been overused in this way, the soil now turned hard and the gardens covered with the thick grass.

Given the definitely limited resources of the island and the absolute and rather low population density supportable under such extensive techniques, the expanding Yapese population would have inevitably reached a point beyond which any attempt to increase productivity under shifting cultivation alone would have become counterproductive. In the resulting context of land pressure the Yapese could have been led to rely increasingly on the intensive techniques of taro cultivation, which could have then, as Alkire describes, both drawn people together in more concentrated settlements about those areas where taro could be grown and allowed a smaller family unit, opening up the way for new forms of social organization.

Irrigated taro farming requires totally different kinds of labor investments from extensive shifting agriculture and thus allows a different organization of the subsistence work force. Whereas shifting agriculture requires repeated major investments of labor as one garden area is allowed to lie fallow and another garden established elsewhere, wet taro farming requires an initial major investment of labor to establish the taro patch in a suitable location with proper irrigation, but then the labor required to maintain the patch and keep it productive—weeding, harvesting, mulching, and replanting—can be effectively done by one person. The rise of taro agriculture thus carried with it the potential for a reduction in the size of the basic subsistence unit, both in the number of persons involved and in the amount of land it required. Once taro patches had been built, the need for a cooperatively organized work force and extensive garden lands would be significantly reduced, individuals being able to maintain themselves independently on specific taro plots, and the matrilineal joint estate could have been easily subdivided and fragmented. This, in turn, could have been seen as especially advantageous in the matrilineal/matrilocal context, allowing a strategic realignment of authority based on new relations of landholding.

In his generalized analysis of the dynamics of matrilineal kinship, Schneider (Schneider and Gough, 1961, pp. 1–29) has shown the difficulty of establishing strong lines of authority and allegiance in a matrilineal/matrilocal system. Since authority over the matriline and its resources remains with its men, a man who marries in and comes to live with his wife usually finds his authority over her and their children distinctly limited. Although he may be allowed some control over domestic affairs, the affairs of his wife's descent group generally will remain under the control of its men, who themselves live elsewhere. At the same time, although he may retain authority over his own descent group, he himself has left it and given up control of at least some of its activities to similar in-marrying men. The arrangement makes it doubly difficult for the men to organize themselves politically. Their matrilineal kinsmen have been dispersed to other estates, and the authority of the in-marrying men living together on any estate is dispersed elsewhere in their own matrilines. It can also easily divide the loyalties of the women and children, who face the demands both of the men of their own descent groups and of the in-marrying men as husbands and fathers. Although it is difficult to tell exactly the process by which this might have changed, it appears from the cultural patterns that emerged that taro production presented the men of the matri-estate an opportunity to consolidate their power, shifting to a pattern of patrilocal residence and patrilineal succession that concentrated about one point the line of men who would exercise authority. This could have been a political necessity. For the same conditions of land pressure that appear to have motivated the shift to taro production would have doubtless also motivated an increase in territorial conflict and rivalry as some groups tried to expand, encouraging the formation of stronger organizations of power.

The mechanism through which the shift from a matrilineal/ matrilocal organization to the estate system took place appears to have been broadly similar to that described by Murdock (1949) in his discussion of bride-price. Murdock argues that where, in a matrilineal society, there develops any form of movable property or wealth that can be concentrated in the hands of men, there tends to be a shift to patrilocal residence and patrilineal inheritance:

> With such property, whether it be herds, slaves, money, or other valuables, prosperous men can offer a bride-price to the parents of girls which will induce them to part with their daughters. The concentration of property in the hands of men specifically facilitates a transition to patrilineal inheritance among peoples who have previously followed the rule of matrilineal inheritance, for men now have the power and the means to make effective their natural preference for transmitting their property to their own sons rather than to their sororal nephews. Warfare, slavery, and political integration all encourage patrilocal residence. War enhances the men's influence and brings them captive (and hence patrilocal) wives and plunder wherewith to buy other women. Slavery provides a mechanism for purchasing women and enforcing patrilocal residence. Political expansion increases the power and prestige of the men and normally establishes a rule of patrilineal succession, both of which favor patrilocal residence [Murdock 1949, p. 207]

Although land is not strictly speaking "movable property," it can become socially movable, readily transferable or negotiable. It is this that appears to have occurred on Yap with the rise of taro cultivation and the dissolution of the historical form of matrilineal productive relations. By reducing the size of the subsistence unit, taro production would have rendered the relations within the joint matrilineal estate superfluous, effectively creating a structural "surplus" of clan land and clan members—land and people that no longer needed to be held together—that could be exchanged with other groups by those who controlled the clan's resources, specifically the clan men, in order to bring their wives to their own natal estates. However, as we have seen, rather than using the

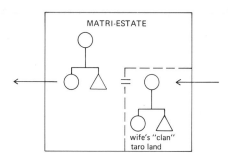

Fig. 36. The movement of women as a man remains on his natal matri-estate

property to compensate the woman's kin group for the loss of her services, the Yapese appear to have used it in a transaction set up directly between the man and his wife and children, a transaction defined not by the "natural preference" of men, but most likely by the possibility of their strengthening their authority in a specific context. In return for the land alienated from the matri-estate, the man and his close matrilineal kin could demand the service and, equally important, the allegiance of the in-marrying clan group. If a son refused his absolute loyalty to his father, he could lose his claim to the land. Whereas authority had previously been diffused as men moved from the estate in which they had authority to estates in which they did not, now they could focus on one estate, demanding unconditional allegiance from those who came to live on it. At the same time, the movement of clan women could conceivably have also been used to create and maintain political alliances between different groups, helping to form the kinds of concentrations of power within and between the growing villages that ultimately led to the Yap-wide war alliances.

By taking the estate relations, then, on their own explicit terms— that is, as relations involving subdivisions of taro-producing land transacted between clan groups—it is possible for us to understand the general relations of clan and estate as relations formed by the Yapese in response to a particular set of objective conditions on Yap. The interaction of clan and estate, the dialectic of people and land that was fundamental to Yapese social relations, now appears as the real historical interaction of the social forms of the early matrilineal society with the changing productive relations of Yapese agriculture. It appears concretely as the land of Yap being adapted to the people in the development of a more productive form of cultivation and the people of Yap being adapted to the land in the development of the social relations of the estate, transforming themselves and their social institutions at the same time as they transformed the land.

But we can take our analysis even further. For the same process that redefined estate relations would also have had other effects. It could redefine the very ideological constructs of "clan" and "estate" themselves, giving them the form we have described. This is evident even at the purely structural level, apart from such causal factors as land pressure and taro production. Through the transactions of land between clan groups, the clan would be set free from its identity with any specific land, while the estate would be set free from its identity with any specific clan. The once indivisibly unified matrilineal "clan-estate" would effectively be deconstituted into the "clan" on the one hand and the "estate" on the other, the clan taken as only a unit of people who were objectively "the people of Yap," those who labored, and the estate as only a unit of land, "the land of Yap," the property that was labored upon.

That it was specifically the *land* of the estate that became the repository of status, clan people "speaking for the land" they held, can also be seen to result from this process. For it was not simply land that would be transacted for service and loyalty, but "clan land," an estate belonging to a clan group with a specific social position, itself passed through the matriline. Clan groups exchanged positions socially as well as physically, giving up the clan position they had held and taking another. The "clan land" would thus be separated from the clan as land or exchangeable property, which itself contained a particular status, a (clan) status that different groups assumed as they replaced their predecessors. While this put new emphasis on the estate, it also, of course, stripped the clan of enduring ties either to land or to status. As all social power came to reside in the estate, specifically in the men who held it, the clan could come to be defined simply as a historical reproductive group, without organization or power, whose main significance was that it contained women, the "resource" that produced men—and more women, the producers of more men.

If we consider this transaction of "clan status" as well as "clan land" in greater detail, we can, I think, also begin to understand still other significant features of Yapese traditional culture, features which may before have appeared purely "symbolic." For it is the transaction of "clan status" as well as "clan land" that in turn seems to account for the all-pervasive scaling of people and land in the system of *tabugul* and *taay*.

Under a matrilineal system where both land and status were passed through the matriline, any particular "sacred" (*tabugul*) status, for example, "chief" or "priest," would remain exclusively within the bounds of one descent group, probably localized at one estate. With the transaction of the estate between clan groups, however, such an exclusive *tabugul* status would be opened up to any clan group that might marry in. Once the notion of *tabugul* ceased to be restricted to specific matrilines, the new process of clan mobility would, in effect, make all clan groups potentially *tabugul:* any clan group could theoretically move from estate to estate over generations, until it arrived at the highest *tabugul* land. Since the status of *tabugul* would no longer be the prerogative of any genealogically bounded group but would be open to anyone who could attain it, the progress of any particular group or person toward that end could be stated in terms of relative *tabugul* status. Those who had progressed closer to establishing themselves on the higher estates would consequently be more *tabugul* than those behind them, who would be comparatively *taay*.

It was, of course, specifically *subsections* of estates that would now have had the qualities of *tabugul* and *taay*. With the transaction between clan groups, the estate would have also been subdivided into land that remained identified with the original clan owners— and their social position—and the land that was alienated to the in-marrying woman and her clan. In cases where the original matriestate was associated with a *tabugul* status, this can easily be seen to lead to a subdivision between land and people that retained that *tabugul* status and land and people that were separated off as *taay*, a term that, as we noted, meant that which was "dirty," having been cast off from the established order. Even where the matri-estate's status was not originally *tabugul*, a similar ranking of estate subsections would occur that could be then subsumed into the notions of *tabugul* and *taay* as they were generalized. At the same time clan land was subdivided, so it appears was clan status (*tabugul*), putting both together on the same continuous scale running throughout Yapese society.

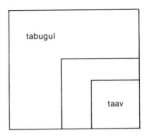

Fig. 37. The subdivision of a *tabugul* matri-estate

We can take this yet a step further. For the process of segregating
the estate into a succession of different *tabugul* and *taay* subdivisions created not simply ranks, but more precisely men's and
women's ranks, the two having different roles within the estate. For
men, who would remain on their natal estate and move up through
it, the different ranked positions created within an estate would be
defined simply by the estate's life cycle, the total number of different
clan groups represented on it at any one time as members of the
oldest groups died and the men of the young groups took new wives.
For women, who moved from their natal estate to a marital estate,
the different ranked positions would be defined both by the estate's
life cycle and by the process of moving from one estate to another.

As we saw, prepubescent girls, *buliel,* were not strictly segregated
into a separate eating class, having not yet attained their "womanhood," and were able to eat with those of other classes. But once a
woman reached puberty, she would automatically enter the rank of
the *rugoth,* which denoted a young and fertile, though as yet child-
less woman, who had become marriageable and was expected to
leave her natal estate but who had not yet established a claim to land
elsewhere. She would remain an essentially unattached *rugoth* even
after marriage, until she produced children and thereby made her
first significant claim on her husband's estate. It was at that point
that she would enter the lowest of four categories defined by the
process of estate transaction. They distinguished the woman who
had successively married onto the estate and produced children,
segregating the women of different clan groups (their food resources,
eating areas, etc.) and explicitly marking the stages in a woman's
own life cycle on the estate: childbearing women (*dien*), fully productive women (*pithorang*), menopausal women (*puweluwol*), and
old women (*pin ni pilibithir*) (fig. 38).

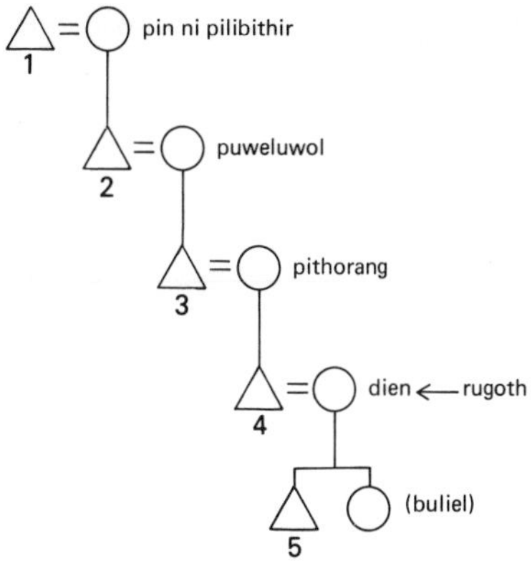

Fig. 38. The formation of the women's ranks

From this structure of women's ranks it appears that the life cycle of the estate was five generations, a depth that indeed seems reasonable, putting its oldest members in their late sixties. Parallel to the women's categories here would thus also be five categories of men who were born on the estate, which I have simply numbered on the diagram. Yet while every estate did distinguish at least that many men's ranks, it will be recalled that the complete system of men's ranks, the *yogum*, comprised not five but seven ranks. This expansion of men's ranks seems to be due to the fact that the *yogum* eating class system was organized on a villagewide basis, including men from estates that were themselves of different rank.

The formal *yogum* men's ranks can be understood as a grouping of people and land of equal status. In its simplest form we can see that the hierarchical rankings within different estates could easily be matched up so that people and land of the same social position would be formed into broad social strata, only those of the same general rank being able to share their food resources and eat together. If all estates had exactly the same social standing, then there would have been only five *yogum* ranks as defined internally within each estate, the men of similar estate positions being ranked together. However, if we assume, as seems reasonable, that the *yogum* system arose in the context of an already existing structure of rank, where estates had different social standings, the seven levels of the *yogum* become quite comprehensible.

If estates were of different ranks, the matching process at the base of the *yogum* would have to take into account both a man's own position within his estate and the position of his estate within the overall village ranking scheme. This could be done quite easily. The second-ranking man of the highest estate could be ranked with the highest-ranking man of a second-ranking estate, the third-ranking man of the highest estate with the second-ranking man of a second-ranking estate, as well as the highest-ranking man of a third-ranking estate, and so on. Given that the estate itself internally distinguished five ranks of men as we saw above, one need only assume three different estate ranks, and this kind of matching would logically produce a seven-strata rank system, as is shown in figure 39. The structure of the *yogum* itself seems to indicate that this was generally how the system was formed.

Estate 1	Estate 2	Estate 3		
1	--		level	1
2	------------------ 1	---	level	2
3	------------------ 2	--------------- 1	----------------	level	3
4	------------------ 3	--------------- 2	----------------	level	4
5	------------------ 4	--------------- 3	----------------	level	5
	------------------ 5	--------------- 4	----------------	level	6
	------------------------------------	--------------- 5	----------------	level	7

Fig. 39. The formation of *yogum* ranks from different level estates

In our previous discussion, we saw that a major structural division within the *yogum* was between the four lower and relatively *taay* eating classes of the "young men" (*pagal*) of the village and the three top *tabugul* classes of the "men" (*pumoon*) of the village. Advancement from the ranks of the "young men" to the ranks of the "men" entailed a fundamental change in a man's social definition and necessitated the special *doach* initiation ceremony (fig. 40). Advancement into a *yogum* rank depended on the possession of the appropriate-level taro patch, each estate consequently being defined by the highest-ranking land it possessed. Only men of the highest estates could advance through all three top levels. Members of estates with lesser authority could advance to the second highest level, and the oldest men of all other estates could reach only the lowest *tabugul* level beyond the *doach* (*beech*). There were thus exactly three ranks of estates within the village, those whose men would attain the highest *tabugul* eating class, those whose men would attain the middle *tabugul* eating class, and those whose men would attain only the lowest *tabugul* eating class.

This ranking of different estates through three "men's" *yogum* ranks can also be seen as a result of the broadening and matching of estate subdivisions. The subdivision of the *yogum* was explicitly phrased as a subdivision into age groups, the "men" who had become *tabugul* through the *yogum* being opposed to the "young men" who remained *taay*. Yet, if taken literally as such, the groupings would really fit only the highest of estates. In the lower estates, where the men could only reach the second- or third-highest eating class, some of those who were generally considered "men" by reason of age and estate position would necessarily remain "young men" in the *yogum*. A man could be in his forties or fifties and exercise most of the authority of his estate yet still be in the lower eating ranks of the "young men," not yet having gone through the *doach.*

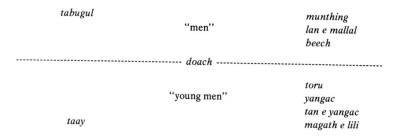

Fig. 40. The separation of *tabugul* "men" and *taay* "young men"

In the highest estates, however, the correspondence between the structure of age and authority and the expressed categories of the *yogum* is so exact that it suggests it was there, in the process of such estates' subdivision, that these *yogum* distinctions were established. There the men of the three senior clan groups would be ranked as "men" in the *yogum,* having gone through the *doach* and taken positions in the top three classes, and would also be considered "men" in the broader meaning of the term, since even the youngest of the three had reached an age when he would have taken some of the authority of the estate. It will be recalled that the structure of authority on the estate was described in terms of the relations of these three men, the oldest male of the estate who could no longer take an active role in its affairs but who most represented its authority, his aging son who directed estate affairs, and his son in turn, who actively carried out the estate's authority. The younger males of the estate, those of the two junior clan groups, were described as having no real authority, though they would do the others' bidding. As their elders were "men" both in age and in *yogum* rank, so they were "young men" both in the sense that they themselves were still young and in the sense that they still remained in the lower *yogum* classes.

While the *yogum* categories fit with the categories of age and authority on a high estate, what specifically segregated the "men" from the "young men" and formed them into separate categories of *tabugul* and *taay* was the *doach*, the initiation ceremony through which males were ritually transformed from being inherently *taay* as "young men" to being inherently *tabugul* as "men." This also makes the most sense in terms of the dynamics of a high estate, especially if we assume that the high estate had originally been associated with a *tabugul* status, an assumption supported by the fact that the highest estates were seen as historically *tabugul*, being something like shrines associated with the founders of Yapese society.

The transaction of an originally *tabugul* matri-estate between clan groups would mean that its authority would be exercised by unrelated men who had not before been identified with its *tabugul* status and may not have been associated with any other *tabugul* status. The *doach* in this context could have been a kind of ritual performed on the historical social order, transferring such non-*tabugul* people into the ranks of the *tabugul* in order to allow them to play a role perhaps once reserved to a specific descent group. As the men of the three leading clan groups of the *tabugul* estate each went through the *doach* in turn and were ceremonially transformed in order to be able to exercise the estate's authority, the males of the estate would be simultaneously differentiated into two categories. The "men" who had become *tabugul* would form one category, and the "young men" who remained *taay* would form the other. Such a high *tabugul* estate would thus be subdivided not only by the structure of successive clan groups, but also by the structure of age and authority on it, both differentiating the clan men and women into ranks and then differentiating the men's ranks themselves.

By so doing, the subdivision in the highest *tabugul* estate would thus form in itself a scale of ranks subordinate to the highest *tabugul* rank to which other estate rank distinctions could be easily shaped by analogy. That all estates were able to attain at least the lowest of the three *tabugul* ranks of the *yogum* suggests that this is exactly what occurred. The ranking sections of estates subordinate to the high estate could simply be equated with an appropriate subordinate subsection of the high estate, giving three levels of estate rank (fig. 41). As has been indicated, this would further have generalized the

other distinctions formed within the highest estate around the
doach. Those grouped with the top, *tabugul* subsections of the high
estate could be thought of as being similarly *tabugul,* themselves
also requiring the ritual transformation of the *doach,* and the set of
broad *tabugul* ranks of "men" separated from the set of broad *taay*
ranks of "young men" throughout the *yogum*. In the context of the
land pressure and intense rivalry that I propose underlay the structural transformations that created the rank system, it is reasonable
to expect that people would have been extremely conscious of any
such status differences as they reflected political power and would
have attempted to assume whatever distinctions of rank they could.

	Estate 1 (*tabugul*)	Estate 2	Estate 3	
tabugul	1			munthing
"men"	2	1		lan e mallal
	3	2	1	beech
-----	-----	-----	---- doach	-----------------
	4	3	2	toru
"young men"	5	4	3	yangach
		5	4	tan e yangach
taay			5	magath e lili

Fig. 41. The ranking of lower estates in relation to a high *tabugul* estate to create the
yogum system.

Having placed the *tabugul/taay* system in the context of the
process of estate transaction, and thereby at least tentatively
accounted for its structure, we can finally understand the particular
meaning carried by the terms themselves. By encompassing the
highest-ranking land and people of even the lowest estates, the
tabugul ranks of the *yogum* came to comprise the land and people
who most directly represented the matri-estates of the matrilineal
order, the highest section of an estate being identified as that from
which all other estate subdivisions had been originally derived. The
tabugul ranks can thus be seen to embody the established order of
recognized matri-estate statuses, the matrilineal social order that
had been the historical source of all estate subdivisions. As a clan
moved from estate to estate, it, or at least its men, would leave that
historical order momentarily, giving up the position attained by the
clan at one estate, and then reenter it at another estate via the *doach*
(re)initiation, in a sense continually going below the established

historical order and resurfacing at a different place with a different status—in a sense reenacting the process by which the society had taken its present form. The terms *tabugul* and *taay* were in effect historical terms. To be *tabugul*, "sacred," "high," "clean," "pure," was not simply to control production, to be the source of productivity (see chap. 5, pp. 71–72), but specifically to control production by becoming more and more part of the historical landowning order; to be *taay* was not simply to lack that control, but similarly to lack control as part of a dependent non-landowning suborder set apart outside the landowning order, historically sectioned off as "profane," "low," "dirty," "impure"—beneath the established society.

This analysis of *tabugul* and *taay* admittedly has dealt only with estate and village rank and not with intervillage rank, which was also structured around the same notions. Intervillage rank was clearly based on the same kind of land relations as the other systems, the *taay* villages of the *pimilingay* being explicitly said to have been sectioned from land of the *tabugul* villages of the *pilung*. Yet too much information is lacking on the nature of the relations between villages for us to see exactly how that system took its formal shape. It is suggestive that its seven-level structure (fig. 42) may have been

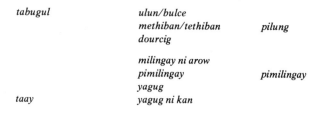

Fig. 42. The ranks of *pilung* and *pimilingay*

exactly like that of the *yogum*, being divided between the three top *tabugul* ranks of those with land and authority, here the *pilung,* and four lower *taay* ranks of those who were dependent on them, being without either authority or land, the *pimilingay*. From this it is not difficult to imagine how the village stratifications could have been formed out of the *yogum* classes following the same sort of logic by which the *yogum* was formed out of the estate ranks. If the men of villages of different political strengths were matched together such that the second-ranking men of the strongest villages were ranked with the top-ranking men of the next strongest villages (and so on),

then there would be the same kind of formalization of village relations as there had been for estate relations. As fig. 43 shows, seven-
level village-rank system would be produced, again internally subdivided between *tabugul* (*pilung*) and *taay* (*pimilingay*). As we noted
in chapter 5, there was a difference between the *yogum* ranks of
different villages, a man of a higher village not being able to eat food
out of the pot of a man of a lower village, even though they had
reached the same *yogum* rank. The people of the *pimilingay* villages
were also said to be able to share the food only of the *pilung* women
and young men, and the lower-ranking *pimilingay* shared the food
only of the lower-ranking *pilung* women. But it is far from clear to
what extent this operated. Again, the context of land pressure and
competition between villages over the control of resources would
have encouraged the discrimination and marking of rank at all
levels, defining which villages had the power to compete politically,
and which could equitably exchange women as well as food. Yet it
is also possible that once discriminations linking the *yogum* structure and village rank had been established, they might not have been
strictly adhered to as what appears to be a fairly dynamic political
situation on Yap changed, some villages losing, others gaining in

	high village yogum		
tabugul	level 1	village 1	
"men"	level 2	village 2	*pilung*
	level 3	village 3	
"young men"	level 4	village 4	
	level 5	village 5	*pimilingay*
	level 6	village 6	
taay	level 7	village 7	

Fig. 43. The formation of *pilung* and *pimilingay* ranks

power. The more loosely knit intervillage relations might have
allowed a degree of flexibility not found within the villages. I present
all of this, however, only in the most tentative way.

What is much clearer with respect to Yapese politics is the connection between the fundamental transactional relations of clan
groups within an estate and the structure of the political leadership.
This connection was explicitly made by the ideology itself, with the
chiefly statuses at all levels being conceived of in estate terms. The

general organization of political leadership was presented, we saw, as a simultaneous development and modification of the estate pattern, an extension of the structure of authority and the relations of production within the estate that created new aggregations of concrete village power and authority as ultimately reflected in the "side of the chiefs" and the "side of the young men"; this seems to fit quite well into the dynamics of the historical situation I have posited.

The shift to predominant taro production not only would have allowed a subdivision of the matri-estate between clan groups and a consequent concentration of political power, but also, it was suggested, would have tended to concentrate population around those specific areas most favorable to taro cultivation, leading to a denser village settlement pattern as the Yapese population continued to expand. It would have thus given rise to localized villages unified under the political authority of the older landholding estates, villages that could have asserted considerable political power. The intensification of agricultural production would have, in effect, led to an intensification of politics, to a new concentration of political as well as productive power. This could not fail to have a profound effect on the political relations between landholding groups. The result would almost surely have been the village-oriented political organization, probably giving rise to the strong district organizations of power under leading local villages.

The creation of such localized aggregations of power was seen to have given the system of political leadership its form. As more estates were established within the villages through estate subdivision among sons, not only were village sections and subsections and their leaders seen to have been produced, but also, at the level of the most powerful villages, the oppositional powers of the *ulun*, the leaders of the "side of the young men." They were specifically seen to have emerged with the growth of village power, their strength being the strength of the massive alliance of villages they headed.

The opposed war alliances of the "side of the chiefs" and the "side of the young men" themselves seem to come to be balanced against each other through this same process of village growth. The development of local village power would have considerably increased the possible scope of conflict between groups as one group attempted to expand its boundaries or prerogatives over another. But at the same time there would be distinct limitations to such conflict. Given the island setting, territorially or politically expansive warfare by one growing political center would soon become disruptive to the society as a whole as groups that lost political power in one direction attempted to regain it from other neighbors. Yap is large enough and its resources are evenly enough distributed that there could have been a fairly even development of localized power centers throughout the island. In such a context, where expansion by one group would tend to upset the balance between others, a kind of alliance system that stabilized the relations between forces through an elaborate system of checks and balances would have kept the distinct localized powers in balance, maintaining the position of the leading villages of both sides and allowing no one village to dominate all others.

Taken as an actual historical process, then, the dialectical interaction of clan and estate can be seen to lay the foundations of the basic structural features of Yapese culture, of the constructs of "clan" and "estate" themselves, of the *tabugul* and *taay* ranks, of the opposed political alliances. In a very real sense, Yapese culture appears to be about that actual historical process, about the relations of people and land as they were defined and redefined in the daily practice of producing subsistence, and ultimately in the particular forms of agriculture upon which Yapese life was predominantly based. The ideology of the dialectic of clan and estate was essentially a statement of the conditions under which the people could continue to maintain themselves from the land, defining the nature of those who themselves labored as well as the nature of the property on which they labored. The system of *tabugul* and *taay* similarly distinguished different kinds of property and property holders, structuring the relations between such persons specifically as such. Yapese culture was, in effect, most explicitly based on property relations, the historically developed social relations of production by which the Yapese had come to sustain themselves from the land. Its categories appear as the categories created by and within those relations, as the categories of a particular concrete historical reality. Its structure appears as the structure not of the human mind, but of human history—the structure of the changing relations through which a people labored to appropriate from nature their means of cultural survival.

Notes

Chapter 1

1. Reported in United States Navy Department (1944). It is unclear whether this figure also includes Chamorros employed on Yap.

Chapter 2

1. The glosses "child," "mother," and "father" should not be taken to mean only ego's actual child, mother, and father. As we shall see later in chapter 4, the terms include others who were also considered "children," "mothers," and "fathers."

2. The only other example of such ownership rights was the breadfruit tree, which sends shoots up from its spreading roots. The new trees also belong to the person who owns the parent tree. In Gagil municipality, they spoke of *welwel likethow,* "following the breadfruit roots," as the relation of two people descended from two sisters through two different lines of females.

3. One person did in fact claim that all estates on Yap of the name *Dacangar* had originally belonged to the Weloy clan, and all estates with names ending in *-fay* had belonged to the Kanfay clan. Other estates were said to belong to a clan as "clan land" (*tafen e ganong*), though not passed along clan lanes, but not much was known about them beyond that.

Chapter 3

1. When the Yapese first made stone money out of the white rock found in Palau, a man from the island of Ulithi was there. When he saw them stick a pole through the center of the disk, he said, *"fae,"* which is the Ulithian word for coitus. The Yapese, of course, didn't know that, but overhearing the word, adopted it for their newly created money. So they say. In Gagil municipality, where Ulithians come to give tribute, stone money is referred to as *ray* out of deference to the visitors.

Chapter 4

1. Not all people remembered the term *wa'ayengin* and, while some applied it to both sister's daughter and sister's son, others said it applied only to sister's son as the reciprocal of same term as it applied to mother's brother. Because it appears to make more sense analytically to apply the term to both sister's daughter and sister's son, I have followed that course here. The term itself was said to refer to a kind of "sibling," and those who did not know it did referred to both mother's brother and sister's child as *wolag,* "sibling."

2. Schneider (1956, chap. 3, p. 18) records a special form of marriage related to this, called *wu:c:* "This occurs when a woman dies in childbirth or shortly thereafter,

leaving an infant or small child. The widower may then go to any single woman, including one of his wife's unmarried sisters, and ask her to come and care for the child. A marriage is only properly termed *wu:c* if it is explicitly undertaken in order to provide care for an infant or small child."

Chapter 5

1. The verb "to crawl" is *gamanaman*. The noun *gamanaman* means "animal," and the verb would thus be "to move like an animal," a concept that certainly fit the social position of the *rugoth*.

2. *Yogum* rank names collected for other areas that seem reliable are as follows. In the starred villages the names were given independently by at least two persons:

*Gacapar village:	*Wonyan village:	*Tab village:
Arow	*Arow*	*Puluy*
Yamey ni pilung	*Munthing*	*Dagucol*
Matha'eg	*Matha'eg*	*Matha'eg*
Yangac	*Yangac*	*Yangac*
Waltharir	*Tathal*	*Lan e mallal*
Racoloy	*Waltharir*	*Tan e lan e mallal*
Puth	*Puth*	*Yothor*

*Balebat village:	Gal' and Dulukan villages:
Munthing	*Talang*
Garkuf/Welu'	*Pimindaraw*
Matha'eg	*Matha'eg*
Pitoru	*Pitoru*
Pagal	*Daco'ay*
Lan e mallal	*Pagal*
Magath e lili	*Magath e lili*

3. In some *pilung* villages, at least, *arow* was also the area where the top three *tabugul* eating classes met on ritual occasions and had their food cooked and served, a fact which reinforces the parallelism in form between the *yogum* levels and the *pilung/pimilingay* village ranks.

Chapter 6

1. See Lingenfelter (1971), Lessa (1950, 1966), and Alkire (1965).

Chapter 7

1. It should be remembered that the estate's "patrilineality" was only in terms of inheritance and authority, not descent; inheritance itself involved a transaction between two different descent groups.

References

Alkire, W. H.
1960   Cultural adaptation in the Caroline Islands. *Journal of the Polynesian Society* 69:123-50.
1965   *Lamotrek Atoll and interisland socioeconomic ties.* Urbana: University of Illinois Press.

Barrau, J.
1961   Subsistence agriculture in Polynesia and Micronesia. *Bishop Museum Bulletin,* no. 223.

Defngin, Francis
1959   Yam cultivation practices and beliefs in Yap. In *Yam cultivation in the Trust Territory,* ed. J. E. de Young. Issued from the office of the Staff Anthropologist Trust Territory of the Pacific Islands, Guam.

Geertz, Clifford
1968   *Agriculture involution: The process of ecological change in Indonesia.* Berkeley: University of California Press, for the Association of Asian Studies.

Gifford, E. W., and Gifford, D. S.
1959   Archaeological excavations in Yap. *Anthropological Records,* vol. 18, no. 2, pp. 149-224.

Hezel, Francis X., S.J.
1970   Spanish Capuchins in the Caroline Islands. *Micronesian Seminar Bulletin.* (Truk, Caroline Islands.)

Johnson, C.; Alvis, R.; and Hetzler, R.
1960   *Military geology of Yap Islands.* Washington, D.C.: U.S. Geological Survey under the direction of the Chief of Engineers, U.S. Army.

Lessa, W.
1950   Ulithi and the outer native world. *American Anthropologist* 52:27-52.

1966   *Ulithi: A Micronesian design for living.* New York: Holt, Rinehart and Winston.

Lingenfelter, S. G.
1971   Political leadership and cultural change in Yap. Ph.D. dissertation, University of Pittsburgh.

Murdock, G. P.
1949   *Social structure.* New York: Macmillan.

⨯ Mahoney, F.
1958   Land tenure patterns on Yap. In *Land tenure patterns in Trust Territory of the Pacific Islands,* ed. J. E. de Young. Issued from the office of the Staff Anthropologist Trust Territory of the Pacific Islands, Guam.

Müller, W.
1917   Yap. In *Ergebnisse der Sudsee-expedition 1908-10,* ed. G. Thilenius, Series 2, Section B, vol. 2, pp. 1-811. Hamburg: L. Friederichsen.

Report of the United Nations Visiting Mission to the Trust Territory of the Pacific Islands, 1970. New York: United Nations Trusteeship Council.

⨯ Schneider, D. M.
1949   The kinship system and village organization of Yap. Ph.D. dissertation, Harvard University.
1953   Yap kinship terminology and kin groups. *American Anthropologist* 55:215-36.
1955   Abortion and depopulation on a Pacific Island. In *Health, culture, and community,* ed. B. Paul. New York: Russell Sage Foundation.
1956   Yap. Unpublished partial manuscript.
1957a   Political organization, supernatural sanctions and the punishment of incest on Yap. *American Anthropologist* 59:791-800.
1957b   Typhoons on Yap. *Human Organization* 16:10-15.
1962   Double descent on Yap. *Journal of the Polynesian Society* 71:1-22.
1967   Depopulation and the Yap *Tabinau.* Mimeographed.
1968   Virgin birth. *Man* 3:126-29.
1969   A Re-analysis of the kinship system of Yap in the light of Dumont's statement. Paper prepared for Burg Wartenstein symposium no. 46, Kinship and Locality.

Schneider, D. M., and Gough, E. Kathleen, eds.
1961   *Matrilineal kinship.* Berkeley: University of California Press.

United States Department of the Navy
1944   *West Caroline Islands.* Civil Affairs Handbook
             (OPNAV 50E-7). Washington, D.C.: Office of the
             Chief of Naval Operations.

Index